My Journey in Faith

Student Response Book

CONCORDIA PUBLISHING HOUSE · SAINT LOUIS

Written by Jill Anthony, Rebecca Brockman, Mark Eiken, Stephen Fehl, Charles and Jeanette Groth, Julie Johnston, Holly Kamprath, James Klawiter, Jim Kroonblawd, Lisa Krenz, James Metcalf, William Moorhead, Beth Orstadt, Eileen Ritter, Darrell Zimmerman

Edited by Rodney L. Rathmann, Kenneth C. Wagener, and Clarence Berndt (2006)

This publication may be available in braille, in large print, or on cassette tape for the visually impaired. Please allow 8 to 12 weeks for delivery. Write to the Lutheran Blind Mission, 7550 Watson Rd., St. Louis, MO 63119-4409; call toll-free 1-888-215-2455; or visit the Web site: www.blindmission.org.

Manufactured in Roanoke, VA / 022100/ 406040

2 3 4 5 6 7 8 9 10 15 14 13 12 11 10

Contents

1. God Creates **5**
The First Article

2. The Fall into Sin **9**
The Seventh Petition

3. God Saves Noah and His Family **12**
The Power of Baptism

4. God Blesses Abraham with Faith **16**
The Third Article

5. God Blesses Jacob **19**
The Fifth and Seventh Commandments

6. God Cares for Joseph **22**
The Sixth Commandment

7. God Calls Moses **25**
The Second Commandment

8. God Delivers His People **29**
The Blessings of Baptism

9. God Leads His People to the Promised Land . . . **32**
The Ninth and Tenth Commandments

10. God Brings Ruth into His Family **38**
The Fourth Commandment
The Close of the Commandments

11. God Promises David a Kingdom **41**
The Fourth Petition

12. God Blesses Solomon **44**
The Third Commandment

13. God Empowers Elijah **47**
The Introduction to the Lord's Prayer and the First Petition
The First Commandment

14. God Preserves His People through Esther **51**
The Eighth Commandment

15. God Restores His People **54**
Luther's Morning and Evening Prayers

16. Jesus' Birth **57**
The Second Article

17. Jesus Is Baptized **60**
What Baptism Indicates

18. Jesus Is Tempted **63**
The Sixth Petition

19. Jesus Calls His Disciples **67**
The Second and Third Petitions

20. Jesus Teaches Nicodemus **71**
The Nature of Baptism

21. Jesus Teaches in Parables **75**
The Fifth Petition

22. Peter Confesses Jesus **79**
The Office of the Keys

23. Jesus Raises Lazarus **83**
The Second Article

24. Jesus Enters Jerusalem **86**
The Conclusion to the Lord's Prayer

25. Jesus the Servant **89**
Confession and Absolution

26. Jesus Gives the Lord's Supper **92**
The Nature and Benefit of the Sacrament of the Altar

27. Jesus Is Condemned and Crucified **97**
The Power of the Sacrament of the Altar
Worthily Receiving the Sacrament

28. Jesus Rises from the Dead **102**
What Baptism Indicates
Law and Gospel

29. Jesus Ascends into Heaven **105**
The Second Article

30. Jesus Sends the Holy Spirit **108**
The Third Article

God Creates

The First Article

I believe in God, the Father Almighty, Maker of heaven and earth.

What does this mean? I believe that God has made me and all creatures; that He has given me my body and soul, eyes, ears, and all my members, my reason and all my senses, and still takes care of them. He also gives me clothing and shoes, food and drink, house and home, wife and children, land, animals, and all I have. He richly and daily provides me with all that I need to support this body and life. He defends me against all danger and guards and protects me from all evil. All this He does only out of fatherly, divine goodness and mercy, without any merit or worthiness in me. For all this it is my duty to thank and praise, serve and obey Him. This is most certainly true.

Who Am I?

- **Complete the following chart to begin your Journey in Faith.**

Full Name: _____

Date of Birth: _____

Place of Birth: _____

Hair Color: _____

School: _____

Favorite Food: _____

Favorite Music: _____

Favorite Movie: _____

The LORD God took the man and put him in the Garden of Eden to work it and take care of it. And the Lord God commanded the man, "You are free to eat from any tree in the garden; but you must not eat from the tree of the knowledge of good and evil, for when you eat of it you will surely die." The LORD God said, "It is not good for the man to be alone. I will make a helper suitable for him." Now the LORD God had formed out of the ground all the beasts of the field and all the birds of the air. He brought them to the man to see what he would name them; and whatever the man called each living creature, that was its name. So the man gave names to all the livestock, the birds of the air and all the beasts of the field.

But for Adam no suitable helper was found. So the LORD God caused the man to fall into a deep sleep; and while he was sleeping, He took one of the man's ribs and closed up the place with flesh. Then the LORD God made a woman from the rib He had taken out of the man, and He brought her to the man. The man said, "This is now bone of my bones and flesh of my flesh; she shall be called 'woman,' for she was taken out of man." For this reason a man will leave his father and mother and be united to his wife, and they will become one flesh.

Genesis 2:15–24

You're in Charge!

1. **How do you** feel when you are in charge?

   _____

   _____

   _____

2. **It's a big** responsibility when you're in charge of someone or something. What rules do you make when you are in charge at home?

   _____

   _____

   _____

3. **God placed Adam** in charge of the Garden of Eden. What were Adam's responsibilities?

   _____

   _____

   _____

   _____

4. **Adam had certain** rules to live by when God left him in charge of the garden. What command did God give to Adam?

   _____

   _____

   _____

   _____

5. **Why is it** hard to follow rules, even when they are good for us?

   _____

   _____

   _____

   _____

"Alissa, we'll be back in about an hour and a half. While we're gone don't go out front, stay off the Internet, and please don't let your little brother zone out on video games. If you need us, call us on our cell phone. Remember, you're in charge."

God made people different from everything else He made. God created Adam in His own image. After the Lord God formed Adam from the dust of the ground, God breathed into him the breath of life. This is how God began all human life. He breathed life into Adam, and man became a living being.

God made our first parents in His own likeness. He made them to know God. He made them holy, which means "set aside for God's purposes," so that they could talk to God and worship Him. Human beings had a likeness to God. The animals did not.

God talked to Adam and Eve about their life with Him. These people spoke together about their work in the garden. They lived in happy relationship with one another. Adam and Eve knew exactly what God wanted them to do. Because they lived with His likeness, they could do His will. They understood God's will and obeyed Him perfectly and cheerfully. They worshiped God with all their heart. They loved each other as God loved them. They basked in the goodness of their existence and in their closeness to God.

Fellowship with God

God wanted people to live in close communion, or relationship, with Him because He had a special purpose for their lives. God made human beings in His image to represent Him on earth. God made men and women so that they could show each other, and all of God's creation, what God is like. God is love.

The Holy Spirit has taught us that sin spoiled God's plan. It ruined His image in us. But in Jesus, God came to make us over into His image once again. Even though the devil and the temptations of this world have a powerful tug on us, the Holy Spirit gives us knowledge of God's love and forgiveness. He turns our hearts to God and develops in us the desire to obey Him. God has promised to restore us to His full image. He does this each day by the working of the Holy Spirit through His Word. His image in us will be fully restored when He takes us to heaven by His grace.

- **Keisha and Shanna** are sitting in the park, talking about Keisha's older sister. "She is going to get an abortion," Keisha says. "It's her life. Having an abortion is like having your appendix out, only it's simpler."

- **Nathan and Kyle** often go to the video store together on Thursday afternoons. The new sales associate doesn't seem to mind what videos they rent. Although they frequently browse the adult section, Nathan and Kyle have never rented a movie from this section. "Pssst," Nathan whispers, "let's get this one." Kyle looks at the cover. He recognizes the title. He knows that the film is violent, sexually explicit, and degrading to women. "Should we?" Nathan asks.

- **During a field trip** to a beautiful state park, some friends from your class begin to break branches off trees and pull up flowers. "It's only sticks and weeds," James says. "Nobody cares."

Fearfully and Wonderfully Made

- **Create a family tree** that identifies the names and birth dates of your relatives going back three generations. Ask your parents to tell you the stories they know, particularly about your grandparents and great-grandparents. Talk about how your family members' experiences have helped to make you who you are today.

- **Plant a creation garden** with your family. Select a special plant for each person in your immediate family. Volunteer to weed, fertilize, and water the garden. Watch the plants grow and bloom. Talk with your family and catechism teachers about the "watering, weeding, and fertilizing" necessary to help you grow and bloom to be the person God planned for you to become in Christ by the power of the Holy Spirit. The plants in your garden that bloom and grow are reminders that we, nurtured by God's Word and Christian people who teach God's Word, grow and bloom in faith and good works by the Spirit's power.

With My Mentor

- **Ask your mentor** to recall times when he/she was taught the theory of evolution. How does this theory differ from Scripture's account of the creation of the world? How did he/she handle these differences? Develop together an answer so that you can confidently share your belief in God's creation event.

- **With your mentor** read the creation story in Genesis 1. Identify how many times the Scripture records the phrase "And God said." Discuss together the incredible creation power present in God's Word.

"I praise You because I am fearfully and wonderfully made; Your works are wonderful, I know that full well."
Psalm 139:14

_____

- **Write a prayer to your Savior God, thanking and praising Him for making you uniquely you.**

_____

_____

_____

_____

_____

_____

Sign: _____

Date: _____

The Fall into Sin

The Seventh Petition

But deliver us from evil.

What does this mean? We pray in this petition, in summary, that our Father in heaven would rescue us from every evil of body and soul, possessions and reputation, and finally, when our last hour comes, give us a blessed end, and graciously take us from this valley of sorrow to Himself in heaven.

Brandon's Temptation

Brandon usually receives A's in class, on occasion a few B's. He has a strong desire to succeed in school. His parents have high expectations.

Tomorrow is the day of his midterm algebra test. As he sits in his room studying, Brandon hears the phone ring. "Hello," he says. It is his best friend, Collin. "I have the answers to the algebra test," Brandon hears him say. "Do you want me to bring a copy over to you?"

Brandon's mind begins to race. Should he take the answers? He actually knows the kinds of questions that will be on the test. But if everyone else has the answers, he might not get as good a grade as the rest of the class, especially if the teacher grades on a curve.

"Hey, are you still there?" Collin asks.

Brandon hesitates. He knows his parents would be disappointed if he doesn't get an A. "Well . . ."

- **What choices does Brandon have?**

- **What do you think is the right thing for Brandon to do?**

- **In what forms does evil come into your life at school? with your friends? at home?**

Now the serpent was more crafty than any of the wild animals the LORD God had made. He said to the woman, "Did God really say, 'You must not eat from any tree in the garden'?" The woman said to the serpent, "We may eat fruit from the trees in the garden, but God did say, 'You must not eat fruit from the tree that is in the middle of the garden, and you must not touch it, or you will die.' " "You will not surely die," the serpent said to the woman. "For God knows that when you eat of it your eyes will be opened, and you will be like God, knowing good and evil." When the woman saw that the fruit of the tree was good for food and pleasing to the eye, and also desirable for gaining wisdom, she took some and ate it. She also gave some to her husband, who was with her, and he ate it. Then the eyes of both of them were opened, and they realized they were naked; so they sewed fig leaves together and made coverings for themselves.

"And I will put enmity between you and the woman, and between your offspring and hers; He will crush your head, and you will strike His heel."

Genesis 3:1–7, 15

A World Now Evil

1. **Think about** *the perfect relationships Adam and Eve enjoyed in Paradise.*

   a. *Their relationship with God*

   b. *Their relationship with each other*

   c. *Their relationship with themselves*

   d. *Their relationship with God's world*

2. **In what ways** *were relationships broken*

   a. *between Adam and Eve and God?*

   _____

   b. *between Adam and Eve?*

   _____

   c. *between Adam and himself? between Eve and herself?*

   _____

   d. *between Adam and Eve and God's world?*

   _____

3. **Not all evil** *comes into our life as a form of a choice. Accidents, illness, and hurts of all kinds result from the fall into sin. What signs of evil and brokenness do you see in our world today?*

   _____

   _____

   _____

In the Garden of Eden, everything was perfect for Adam and Eve. Their environment and their relationship with God were perfect. They talked with God and enjoyed His blessings. They were content as they trusted and obeyed Him.

Then Satan used the serpent for his evil ends. He convinced Eve that she was right in doubting God's command. Satan used Eve to tempt Adam. Together, Adam and Eve made choices that were contrary to God's commands. They chose to follow their own wishes, as if they were God. They turned against God in selfish pride and unbelief. They had known God's goodness. Now they found out that evil wasn't so good.

After they disobeyed God, Adam and Eve were afraid. Their eyes were opened, as the serpent said they would be. But what did they see? They saw their guilt before God. They had robbed themselves of perfect communion with God. Now they were under God's judgment.

Delivered from Evil

Since the fall, all people are sinful. Now sin is part of our fallen human nature. Sin separates us from God.

We are no better than Adam and Eve. We have tried to take God's place too. We try to be equal with Him. Sin is the cause of misery and unhappiness in the world. It makes us unhappy too. When we are separated from God, we can only turn good to evil. We regularly are forced to battle the devil, the world, and our sinful flesh. Sometimes they gain control in our lives. We sin.

But God offers forgiveness to cancel our sin. In love, He gave His Son, Jesus, to die for us. Through Jesus, God brings us back again into a renewed relationship with Himself. He forgives our sins and equips us with His power to face evil head-on, knowing Jesus has already defeated it at Calvary.

We are His children in Christ!

- **What forces of evil trouble me most right now?**

  _____

  _____

  _____

- **What does Jesus promise me when I am tempted or face evil in other forms?**

  _____

  _____

  _____

- **How will God help me to trust in Him when I am faced with troubles and temptations?**

  _____

  _____

  _____

Sign: _____

Date: _____

Talk about it — With My Family

- **Ask members** of your family to jot down three evidences of Satan's influence that appear on television during the week. Discuss your findings, and pray for God's strength to withstand the temptations of the devil, the world, and our sinful nature that some shows on TV present.

- **God's Word helps** us resist giving in to evil and temptation. Have members of the family share one or more Bible passages that are helpful to them as they face daily life in our sinful world.

With My Mentor

- **Spend some time** with your mentor pulling weeds out of a garden or yard. Talk about how sin has permeated God's creation. Pray together, thanking God for the deliverance He provides in Christ Jesus.

- **Go to the grocery** store with your mentor and purchase fruit to create a fruit basket. Talk about how God's Spirit helps us to resist the forces of evil and to bear fruit in the lives we live for Jesus. Deliver this basket to a shut-in member of your church.

God Saves Noah and His Family

Then God said to Noah and to his sons with him: "I now establish My covenant with you and with your descendants after you and with every living creature that was with you—the birds, the livestock and all the wild animals, all those that came out of the ark with you—every living creature on earth. I establish My covenant with you: Never again will all life be cut off by the waters of a flood; never again will there be a flood to destroy the earth." And God said, "This is the sign of the covenant I am making between Me and you and every living creature with you, a covenant for all generations to come: I have set My rainbow in the clouds, and it will be the sign of the covenant between Me and the earth. Whenever I bring clouds over the earth and the rainbow appears in the clouds, I will remember My covenant between Me and you and all living creatures of every kind. Never again will the waters become a flood to destroy all life. Whenever the rainbow appears in the clouds, I will see it and remember the everlasting covenant between God and all living creatures of every kind on the earth."

Genesis 9:8–16

The Power of Baptism

How can water do such great things? Certainly not just water, but the word of God in and with the water does these things, along with the faith which trusts this word of God in the water. For without God's word the water is plain water and no Baptism. But with the word of God it is a Baptism, that is, a life-giving water, rich in grace, and a washing of the new birth in the Holy Spirit, as St. Paul says in Titus chapter three: "He saved us through the washing of rebirth and renewal by the Holy Spirit, whom He poured out on us generously through Jesus Christ our Savior, so that, having been justified by His grace, we might become heirs having the hope of eternal life. This is a trustworthy saying." [Titus 3:5–8]

What's the Use?

- **Your garden is dry and withering.**
- **A friend encourages you to go off the high dive.**
- **You're thirsty.**
- **The river by your farm rises quickly from the melting snow.**
- **Your school picnic is rained out.**
- **Somebody "hits" you with a supersoaker.**
- **Your pastor baptizes a new baby at church.**

What do you notice in these scenes? Water! Water is a blessing—to drink, to replenish the ground, to enjoy on a hot summer day. On occasion water can be irritating. At times it can be downright scary. Water has many uses in our life. What uses of water does God provide for our physical life? for our spiritual life?

Noah's Story

After the fall of humanity into sin, people no longer put God and His will first in their lives. Instead, they replaced God with their selfish desires and actions. Eventually the Earth became a very violent place, and God was grieved. He planned a great flood to destroy everything except for righteous Noah and his family. These people, eight in all, God saved in a remarkable way. God's saving of Noah and his family remind us of the salvation God provides us through the waters of Baptism. Read the story below, taken from Genesis 6–8.

Noah was a righteous man, and he walked with God. So God said to Noah, "I am going to put an end to all people, for the earth is filled with violence because of them. So make yourself an ark. I am going to bring floodwaters on the earth. Everything on earth will perish, but I will establish My covenant with you, and you will enter the ark—you and your sons and your wife and your sons' wives with you. You are to bring into the ark two of all living creatures, male and female, to keep them alive with you. You are to take every kind of food that is to be eaten for you and for them." Noah did everything just as God commanded him. Then the Lord shut him in.

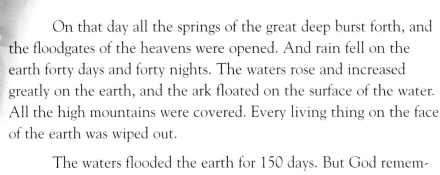

On that day all the springs of the great deep burst forth, and the floodgates of the heavens were opened. And rain fell on the earth forty days and forty nights. The waters rose and increased greatly on the earth, and the ark floated on the surface of the water. All the high mountains were covered. Every living thing on the face of the earth was wiped out.

The waters flooded the earth for 150 days. But God remembered Noah, and He sent a wind over the earth, and the waters receded. The ark came to rest on the mountains of Ararat. The waters continued to recede until the earth was completely dry.

Then God said to Noah, "Come out of the ark." So Noah came out, together with his sons and his wife and his sons' wives. All the animals came out of the ark, one kind after another. Then Noah built an altar to the Lord and sacrificed burnt offerings on it.

Sin, Punishment, and Grace

When people do what they want to do and care nothing about God or His will, they can expect the judgment of God. When people turn away from God and refuse to be called back, they can expect Him to be angry. By our sin, we separate ourselves from God. We go our own way.

Noah was not a perfect man, anymore than we are perfect. He deserved punishment for his sin. But God loved Noah and rescued him. God saved Noah with the waters of the flood. These waters remind us of the waters of Baptism, through which God's Spirit imparts saving grace. By saving Noah and his family, God shows us that He is still working His plan to save sinners. God revealed this plan to all people in Jesus, His Son. Jesus is the great Rescuer. All who trust in Him receive God's mercy. For Jesus' sake, we are forgiven!

Water with a Purpose

When God sent the waters of the great flood, He was both condemning sin and bringing salvation. Explain.

When God works in the waters of Holy Baptism, He is both condemning sin and bringing salvation. Explain.

Rainbow Connections

The rainbow is a reminder to us and to all the world that God keeps His promises. Among these are the promises He makes to us in our Baptism. God promises to continue to bless and keep us in faith as members of His family, to forgive our sins for Jesus' sake, and to remain with us until He comes to take us to live with Him in heaven.

Reflect for a moment on God blessings and promises in your life.

- **I remember God's love when, in the past, He . . .**

_____

- **I'll remember His promises in the future when . . .**

_____

Sign: _____

Date: _____

With My Family

- **Peter associated** Noah's rescue in the flood with Baptism (1 Peter 3:18–22). What benefits are received in Baptism? Ask your parents or brothers and sisters to recall any special family activities from the day of your Baptism. How was your Baptism celebrated? Why were those activities chosen to celebrate your Baptism?

- **If your family** celebrates your Baptism birthday, ask them to tell you why they celebrate. If they don't, encourage your family to think about why and how you might celebrate your Baptism birthday and other Baptism birthdays in your family.

With My Mentor

- **Ask your mentor** to share with you a memorable experience having to do with water. Talk about ways that God's relationship with His creation was reflected in the experience.

- **Ask your mentor** to tell you about a building in town that was torn down. Are there any special memories connected with it? Reflect together about change and how it affects us. Think of the great changes the flood caused for Noah and his family, as well as all of creation. How do you think Noah handled such change? How would you handle such change?

God Blesses Abraham with Faith

The Third Article

I believe in the Holy Spirit, the holy Christian church, the communion of saints, the forgiveness of sins, the resurrection of the body, and the life everlasting. Amen.

What does this mean? I believe that I cannot by my own reason or strength believe in Jesus Christ, my Lord, or come to Him; but the Holy Spirit has called me by the Gospel, enlightened me with His gifts, sanctified and kept me in the true faith. In the same way He calls, gathers, enlightens, and sanctifies the whole Christian church on earth, and keeps it with Jesus Christ in the one true faith. In this Christian church He daily and richly forgives all my sins and the sins of all believers. On the Last Day He will raise me and all the dead, and give eternal life to me and all believers in Christ. This is most certainly true.

Better Than Hoped For

"But, Dad," Brad moaned, "the game starts in an hour, and you promised that we could watch it together! You promised!" Brad's father gave him a quiet smile and calmly said to Brad, "I remember my promise, son. You'll just have to trust me. Come with me."

Brad reluctantly climbed into the car with his dad. As they drove, Brad slumped down in the seat. He was clearly disappointed. The game would start soon, and they were just beginning their errands. He had been waiting for this day for weeks. Just the other day, his dad had promised him again that they could watch the game together.

After this, the word of the LORD came to Abram in a vision: "Do not be afraid, Abram. I am your shield, your very great reward." But Abram said, "O Sovereign LORD, what can You give me since I remain childless and the one who will inherit my estate is Eliezer of Damascus?" And Abram said, "You have given me no children; so a servant in my household will be my heir."

Then the word of the LORD came to him: "This man will not be your heir, but a son coming from your own body will be your heir." He took him outside and said, "Look up at the heavens and count the stars—if indeed you can count them." Then He said to him, "So shall your offspring be." Abram believed the LORD, and He credited it to him as righteousness.

Genesis 15:1–6

Brad's father seemed to be driving without getting anywhere. Brad started to wonder what sorts of errands they had to take care of today. He began to wonder if his dad really understood what a kid needs. Just as he had given up on making it home in time, Brad looked out the window. He saw the stadium a few blocks away. He looked over just as his dad was pulling two tickets out of his shirt pocket. "Box seats, Brad, right behind the dugout! Let's go watch the game!"

- **Describe Brad's feelings when he climbed into the car.**

  _____

- **What might Brad have thought about his father while driving on their "errands"? What did Brad learn about his father?**

  _____

- **In what ways was Brad's day better than what he had hoped for?**

  _____

The ability to trust in God comes as the Holy Spirit works through the means of grace, God's Word and the Sacraments.

The Word of Life

God found Abraham. Abraham did not find God by looking for Him in different places. Abraham did not climb up to God; God came to Abraham. He took Abraham to Himself in love and forgiveness. His Holy Spirit worked faith in Abraham, who had done nothing to make himself worthy of being chosen by God. In mercy, God chose him. God made a covenant of grace with Abraham to send a Savior for all people.

- **What were Abraham and Sarah "missing" in their life?**

  _____

- **Why was Abraham worried about their future?**

  _____

- **What promise did God give Abraham? How did God illustrate His promise to Abraham?**

  _____

- **How would you describe Abraham's faith?**

  _____

Against all hope, Abraham in hope believed and so became the father of many nations, just as it had been said to him, "So shall your off-spring be." Without weakening in his faith, he faced the fact that his body was as good as dead—since he was about a hundred years old—and that Sarah's womb was also dead. Yet he did not waver through unbelief regarding the promise of God, but was strengthened in his faith and gave glory to God, being fully persuaded that God had power to do what He had promised. This is why "it was credited to him as righteousness." The words "it was credited to him" were written not for him alone, but also for us, to whom God will credit righteousness—for us who believe in Him who raised Jesus our Lord from the dead. He was delivered over to death for our sins and was raised to life for our justification.

Romans 4:18–25

God Keeps His Promises

God gave Abraham faith to believe His promises. So Abraham followed God into a new and strange country. Many times Abraham and Sarah were afraid and worried. They did not always trust God. God frequently came to them with a new promise that would strengthen their love for Him. God wanted them to believe what He said and to follow where He led.

God called Abraham to follow Him. God's Spirit created faith in Abraham, and Abraham became a part of God's kingdom.

- **What promises has God spoken to you?**

_____

- **In what ways has God kept His promises to you?**

_____

Growing in Faith and Obedience

God called Abraham and richly blessed Abraham and Sarah. To strengthen their faith, God proved His love over and over again.

God does the same for you. God called you and made you His own in Holy Baptism. Though you deserve His punishment because of your sins, God in mercy chose you to receive eternal life in Jesus, our Savior. He adopted you into His covenant of grace, making you a member of His kingdom. He blesses you in many ways.

Abraham made plenty of mistakes along the way, but God's love for him, promised in the covenant, was steady and sure. God never gave up on Abraham. In spite of your sin and shortcomings, He will never give up on you!

Spend some time talking to God about His patient love for you.

- **God, sometimes I have doubts about . . .**

_____

- **God, sometimes I am afraid of . . .**

_____

- **Yet I believe Your promise that . . .**

_____

Sign: _____

Date: _____

(Talk about it) With My Family

- **Abraham loved** his son. He also trusted God to help him raise Isaac. Ask your parents, "What things do you most want for me? What blessing of the Holy Spirit would you most like for me to possess?"

- **Discuss with your** family the challenges of trusting God. Write a prayer together, asking God for faith as you trust God to help you with a problem you are having in your family right now. Remember to pray the prayer each day this week.

With My Mentor

- **Ask your mentor,** "In the past year, what has been one new way in which God has strengthened your trust in Him? How do you know when God is asking you to follow Him? As you grow older, do you find it easier or more difficult to trust and follow God?"

- **Talk together** about how the Holy Spirit works in believers the desire and motivation to love and obey God. With your mentor discover a new area of obedience that you could work on. Be sure to talk about how Jesus' love and forgiveness helps us as we are forgiven for today's sins and as we learn to be more trusting tomorrow.

God Blesses Jacob

The Fifth Commandment

You shall not murder.

What does this mean? We should fear and love God so that we do not hurt or harm our neighbor in his body, but help and support him in every physical need.

The Seventh Commandment

You shall not steal.

What does this mean? We should fear and love God so that we do not take our neighbor's money or possessions, or get them in any dishonest way, but help him to improve and protect his possessions and income.

So Hungry!

"I'm starvin'!" Have you ever said that? When are you hungriest? Just before lunch? Right after school? Late at night?

One thing is certain: everyone gets hungry. Our bodies need daily nourishment. You may be simply sitting at your desk finishing a math assignment. Or you may be practicing a tough new drill or routine for your team. Either way, when your body is working, it needs nourishment.

Sometime soon you'll need to eat!

• **What kinds of food do you like most?**

Breakfast: _____

Lunch: _____

Dinner: _____

1. **Read Genesis 25:29–34.** *How did Jacob once take advantage of Esau's hunger?*

2. **According to the Fifth** Commandment, *what would God have you do if someone around you is hungry?*

Then Rebekah took the best clothes of Esau her older son, which she had in the house, and put them on her younger son Jacob. She also covered his hands and the smooth part of his neck with the goatskins. Then she handed to her son Jacob the tasty food and the bread she had made. He went to his father and said, "My father." "Yes, my son," he answered. "Who is it?" Jacob said to his father, "I am Esau your firstborn. I have done as you told me. Please sit up and eat some of my game so that you may give me your blessing." Isaac asked his son, "How did you find it so quickly, my son?" "The LORD your God gave me success," he replied. Then Isaac said to Jacob, "Come near so I can touch you, my son, to know whether you really are my son Esau or not." Jacob went close to his father Isaac, who touched him and said, "The voice is the voice of Jacob, but the hands are the hands of Esau." He did not recognize him, for his hands were hairy like those of his brother Esau; so he blessed him. "Are you really my son Esau?" he asked. "I am," he replied. Then he said, "My son, bring me some of your game to eat, so that I may give you my blessing." Jacob brought it to him and he ate; and he brought some wine and he drank. Then his father Isaac said to him, "Come here, my son, and kiss me."

Genesis 27:15–26

I'm Isaac.
My wife, Rebekah, and I believe in God.

We trust His Word. He promised us a son, and we waited for God to fulfill His Word at the right time. Our God, in His mercy, blessed us twice—with twins. Unfortunately, only one could receive the blessing of being the ancestor of God's Messiah. Who would it be—Esau, the older, or Jacob, the younger? Usually the oldest son in a family received the blessing.

As our boys grew, Esau became a skillful hunter. He liked to be outdoors. He and I enjoyed hunting together. Later on, he brought me meat from his hunting. Jacob was a quiet boy. He preferred to stay at home. I came to like Esau better, and Rebekah favored Jacob.

Rebekah wanted Jacob to receive my blessing. She was afraid I would give my blessing to Esau. With Jacob, she planned to trick me. By then I was old and almost blind. She prepared a meal like Esau does. Then she dressed Jacob in Esau's clothes and put animal skins on his arms. I fell for it and gave Jacob my blessing.

When Esau found out about it, he hated Jacob for taking my blessing. He wanted to kill his brother. I knew it was time for Jacob to go away. With Rebekah's help, Jacob left for a distant land where some of our relatives live—the country where our ancestors lived long ago. Before Jacob left, though, I renewed the blessing:

"May God Almighty bless you and make you fruitful and increase your numbers until you become a community of peoples." Genesis 28:3

1. How would you *describe the relationship between Jacob and Esau?*

———————————————
———————————————
———————————————

2. In what ways *is Isaac's family similar to families today?*

———————————————
———————————————
———————————————

3. Was Jacob right? *Was Esau right?*

———————————————
———————————————
———————————————

4. How were the *Fifth and Seventh Commandments broken in this story?*

———————————————
———————————————
———————————————

Where Is God?

Esau and Jacob were brothers, but they were also rivals. They both wanted the blessing from their father. Jacob, with the help of his mother, cheated Esau out of the blessing. That was wrong: they lied. Where was God?

At times, Esau was a selfish, reckless man. One time, when he was hungry, he traded his birthright—his right to the inheritance of the firstborn son—to Jacob for some of Jacob's stew. Esau later wanted to kill Jacob for deceiving their father and getting the blessing. That was wrong: he sinned against the Fifth Commandment—*You shall not murder*. Where was God?

Jacob and Rebekah also sinned. They deceived Isaac into thinking Jacob was Esau. They lied and deceived to steal something and sinned against the Seventh and Eighth Commandments. Jacob, Esau, and Rebekah all sinned against the Fourth Commandment. In fact, none in the family obeyed the First Commandment by letting God keep His promise in His own way. Where was God in all this?

God was right there. He knows how selfish, jealous, and unfaithful people are. Yet God does not allow sin to stand in the way of His plan to save His people. His blessing is always a gift of grace. No one can earn His blessing. God blesses us because He loves us. In mercy, God chose Jacob to be the ancestor of the Savior. Jacob heard God's promise: "I am with you and will watch over you wherever you go, and I will bring you back to this land. I will not leave you until I have done what I have promised you" (Genesis 28:15). God's promise guided and comforted Jacob throughout his life. After wrestling with God just before his return to his homeland, Jacob received a new name from God: *Israel*. Israel means "he struggles with God." From Jacob's family, God continued His promise to save His people by sending the Messiah, Jesus, the Savior of the world. God is with us in Christ!

- **Thank You, Lord! I am thankful You are with me when . . .**

_____

_____

_____

Sign: _____

Date: _____

With My Family

- **Which members** of your family have forgiven each other lately? With your family, take time to ask God for His forgiveness in Christ, to hear His forgiveness in Christ, to hear His assurance of forgiveness in Colossians 1:13–14, and to forgive one another in Jesus.

- **As a family,** write a brief note to relatives you have not seen recently. Include a prayer for God's blessings.

With My Mentor

- **Ask your mentor** how he or she handled family conflict as a young person. Discuss ways to reduce conflict among brothers or sisters or other family members. Brainstorm ways to help and befriend others in keeping the Fifth and Seventh Commandments.

- **Together read** Ephesians 4:32. Describe how God would have us act toward others in keeping the Fifth and Seventh Commandments.

6 God Cares for Joseph

The Sixth Commandment

You shall not commit adultery.

What does this mean? We should fear and love God so that we lead a sexually pure and decent life in what we say and do, and husband and wife love and honor each other.

Headline News

What if Joseph were alive today? The events of his life would make a thrilling story, reported in papers, on TV, and on the Internet.

- **Fill in the headlines** .below with the three key events of Joseph's story in Genesis 37.

Resisting Temptation to Sin Sexually

So Joseph went after his brothers and found them near Dothan. But they saw him in the distance, and before he reached them, they plotted to kill him. "Here comes that dreamer!" they said to each other. "Come now, let's kill him and throw him into one of these cisterns and say that a ferocious animal devoured him. Then we'll see what comes of his dreams." When Reuben heard this, he tried to rescue him from their hands. "Let's not take his life," he said. "Don't shed any blood. Throw him into this cistern here in the desert, but don't lay a hand on him." Reuben said this to rescue him from them and take him back to his father. So when Joseph came to his brothers, they stripped him of his robe—the richly ornamented robe he was wearing—and they took him and threw him into the cistern. . . .

When the Midianite merchants came by, his brothers pulled Joseph up out of the cistern and sold him for twenty shekels of silver to the Ishmaelites, who took him to Egypt.

In His perfect plan, God designed sexual intercourse for a man and woman to experience within marriage. The invitations to sin sexually can make their way into our daily lives just as they came

Continued on page 23

daily to Joseph as he served in Potiphar's house. But Joseph remembered God and His will as he faced these temptations to break the Sixth Commandment. God would have young people today resist sexual temptations just as Joseph did. What role does each of the following have in helping us deal with these temptations?

- **Christ's love for; your trust in Him**

  _____

  _____

- **Talking to a trusted confidant who also loves and trusts in Jesus**

  _____

  _____

- **The Sacraments**

  _____

  _____

God with Me
God is present . . .

God was with Joseph throughout his life, even when he was taken to Egypt. When Joseph sinned, God forgave him. He kept his faith strong through all kinds of hardships. In faith and love, Joseph served the living God until the day of his death.

God has made us His children through His love and mercy in Christ. Jesus has taken away our sins by His death on the cross. He has won the victory over death by His resurrection. We share in His blessings through our Baptism. He is with us every day, keeping us safe in His love and care.

Continued

The Lord was with Joseph in Egypt. The Ishmaelites sold Joseph to Potiphar, one of Pharaoh's officials, and Potiphar put Joseph in charge of everything he owned.

Joseph was handsome and well built. Potiphar's wife was attracted to Joseph. Day after day she flirted with Joseph, asking him to have sex with her. But Joseph refused. "How then could I do such a wicked thing and sin against God?" Joseph said. To get back at Joseph, Potiphar's wife accused Joseph of sexual impropriety (ironically, the very thing she herself was desiring), and Potiphar threw Joseph into prison.

God gave Joseph the ability to interpret dreams. Though he asked Pharaoh's butler to remember him when released from prison, the butler forgot about Joseph until the time when Pharaoh had a troubling dream. Then Joseph was retrieved from prison to interpret the dream. In an amazing turn of events, Joseph became ruler of Egypt, second only to Pharaoh. In this position, Joseph rescued his family, including the very brothers who had sold him, from starvation by bringing them to Egypt.

From Genesis 39–45

Always Near

The LORD, is my shepherd, I shall not be in want.
He makes me lie down in green pastures,
He leads me beside quiet waters, He restores my soul.
He guides me in paths of righteousness for His name's sake.
Even though I walk through the valley of the shadow of death,
I will fear no evil, for You are with me; Your rod and Your staff,
they comfort me. You prepare a table before me in the presence
of my enemies. You anoint my head with oil; my cup overflows.
Surely goodness and love will follow me all the days of my life,
and I will dwell in the house of the Lord forever. (Psalm 23)

With My Family

- **Ask your family** members to share a time that God has worked for good in a bad situation.

- **God has reserved** sexual intercourse for husbands and wives, enabling couples to have a family. As you look through a family photo album together, talk about ways God has cared for your family in both good times and bad times.

With My Mentor

- **Ask your mentor** to share a Scripture verse or story that is especially comforting in times of trouble or temptation.

- **Work with your mentor** to keep a prayer journal for the next week. In your journal, discuss your troubles and temptation. At the end of the week, reflect on the journal with your mentor and see how God has cared for you.

Share right now with your loving Lord any worries or problems you are experiencing, including those relating to sexual temptation. Thank Him for taking your burdens and caring for you.

_____

_____

_____

_____

_____

_____

_____

_____

_____

_____

God Calls Moses

The Second Commandment

You shall not misuse the name of the Lord your God.

What does this mean? We should fear and love God so that we do not curse, swear, use satanic arts, lie, or deceive by His name, but call upon it in every trouble, pray, praise, and give thanks.

Who Would Be You?

Jenny's mother picked her up at Ericka's house. Jenny had spent the night with her friend.

"Did you have fun with Ericka?" Mom asked as they drove toward home.

"We had lots of fun," said Jenny. "Ericka had this book of names. We talked about what names mean and who we'd like to be. At first I wanted to be Miss Desmond, my teacher. Did you know her name, Caitlyn, means 'pure beauty'?"

"Then?" her mother asked.

"After Ericka said she wanted to be the woman who won the gold medal for skating, I changed my mind. I want to be a tennis player and win a gold medal."

Her mom laughed. "It's fun to play pretend, but I want you to be you."

"What do you mean?" asked Jenny.

"If you were Miss Desmond, or if you were a famous tennis player, then I wouldn't have you. When I say 'Jenny,' I think of you. I want you to be who you are because you are very special to me, and to lots of other people too."

Jenny sat quietly for awhile. "I like being me too," she said.

- **What does your name mean?**

_____

- **What meaning have you given to your name?**

_____

When the LORD saw that [Moses] had gone over to look [at the burning bush], God called to him from within the bush, "Moses! Moses!" And Moses said, "Here I am." "Do not come any closer," God said. "Take off your sandals, for the place where you are standing is holy ground." Then He said, "I am the God of your father, the God of Abraham, the God of Isaac and the God of Jacob." At this, Moses hid his face, because he was afraid to look at God.

The LORD said, "I have indeed seen the misery of My people in Egypt. I have heard them crying out because of their slave drivers, and I am concerned about their suffering. So I have come down to rescue them from the hand of the Egyptians and to bring them up out of that land into a good and spacious land, a land flowing with milk and honey—the home of the Canaanites, Hittites, Amorites, Perizzites, Hivites and Jebusites. And now the cry of the Israelites has reached Me, and I have seen the way the Egyptians are oppressing them. So now, go. I am sending you to Pharaoh to bring My people the Israelites out of Egypt."

But Moses said to God, "Who am I, that I should go to Pharaoh and bring the Israelites out of Egypt?"

And God said, "I will be with you. And this will be the sign to you that it is I who have sent you: When you have brought the people out of Egypt, you will worship God on this mountain."

Exodus 3:4–12

God Calls

God Reveals Himself as

Moses responds by

GOD Commands Moses

God Promises Moses

Moses Responds

The people of Israel enjoyed living in Egypt while Joseph ruled. After many years went by, pharaohs ruled who did not remember what Joseph had done. The Egyptians became worried and jealous of the influence of the large and growing group of Israelites. They made the Israelites do hard work. As their situation changed, God always knew of the trials of the children of Israel and never forgot His covenant promises.

God called Moses to deliver His people. God had prepared him for this important work. Moses had received an education as an Egyptian prince; he also had learned how to live in the wilderness. Most of all, Moses had learned to trust in the Lord for strength and wisdom.

The Strong Name

God's Names I Use	God's Power I See	God's Love I Feel	God's Forgiveness I Know

When God told Moses His name, He revealed much about Himself to Moses. God's name is God Himself. God's name, I AM, means that God is eternally existent. He is the Creator of all life and Ruler over all people and all things. God never changes. He keeps all His promises. When he spoke to Pharaoh, Moses would bring the word of the highest Ruler.

God made Moses His spokesman. Moses stood between Israel and the Lord. When the people sinned, Moses told them of God's judgment. When they repented, Moses spoke God's Word of forgiveness. Moses was the one who continually reminded the people of God's faithfulness to the covenant He had made with them.

When God sent His Son, Jesus, He sent the perfect Spokesman. Jesus is the Mediator between God and humanity. By His life, death, and resurrection, Jesus delivers the Gospel of eternal salvation, seals our rescue from sin and death, and displays the faithfulness of God. He prays to God for us.

GOD

- **Ask your older** brother or sister, or another person, about the people in his or her life who were encouragers in the faith. Ask what these encouragers did or said that was helpful as they were growing up. How did these people help them keep the Second Commandment?

- **At your Baptism,** God's name was applied to you together with water. Ask your parents about your Baptism sponsors. Ask why your parents chose them to be your sponsors and encouragers. Write, telephone, or e-mail your sponsors, thanking them for their prayers and encouragement during your journey in faith. Ask them to continue to pray for you as you get older, make more decisions on your own, and grow in your Christian faith.

With My Mentor

- **Talk about** one or more of the persons who have helped you on your journey in faith. Share a way you could be an encourager to her or him in the faith. Pray for growth in Christ. Praise and give thanks to God for that person's influence in your life.

- **Pray together,** thanking and praising God for His holy name and for its meaning in your life.

God's name makes Him real to us. When you call on God's name, you deal with God Himself.

Out of respect for God and what He has done for us through Jesus, God's people use God's name with respect and awe. When we think of God's great love for us, we do not want to speak God's name in a frivolous way or in anger.

We praise God that His name is *Savior*. Because of our sinful ways, we really deserve His anger and punishment. Just as Moses mediated between God and Israel, reminding God that the Israelites were His chosen people and reminding the people of God's grace and mercy, so Jesus stands between God and us. Jesus is our Mediator; He is our Lord and Redeemer from all our sin.

With Respect to God's Name

Review the Second Commandment. In the blanks below on the left, list ways people dishonor God with respect to His holy name. In the blanks below on the right, list ways God commands His people to honor His name.

We misuse God's name when we	**We honor God's name when we**
_____	_____
_____	_____
_____	_____

Write a prayer asking God to help you to honor His name in the life you live for Him.

_____

_____

_____

Sign: _____

Date: _____

God Delivers His People

The Blessings of Baptism

What benefit does Baptism give? It works forgiveness of sins, rescues from death and the devil, and gives eternal salvation to all who believe this, as the words and promises of God declare.

Which are these words and promises of God? Christ our Lord says in the last chapter of Mark: "Whoever believes and is baptized will be saved, but whoever does not believe will be condemned." [Mark 16:16]

Impassable!

"Your room is impassable," Mother sighed.

"You mean *impossible*," Li replied.

"No," Mom said. "I mean *impassable*. I can't get through to the other side."

Like a road covered by water, sometimes life seems impassable. Roadblocks, obstacles, problems. You can't get through a homework assignment. You can't finish a special project. You had an argument with your best friend. You're not certain what to do about a problem.

What "roadblocks" do you face at school? What obstacles might you face in the future?

Moses answered the people, "Do not be afraid. Stand firm and you will see the deliverance the LORD will bring you today. The Egyptians you see today you will never see again. The LORD will fight for you; you need only to be still." . . . Then Moses stretched out his hand over the sea, and all that night the LORD drove the sea back with a strong east wind and turned it into dry land. The waters were divided, and the Israelites went through the sea on dry ground, with a wall of water on their right and on their left. The Egyptians pursued them, and all Pharaoh's horses and chariots and horsemen followed them into the sea. During the last watch of the night the LORD looked down from the pillar of fire and cloud at the Egyptian army and threw it into confusion. He made the wheels of their chariots come off so that they had difficulty driving. And the Egyptians said, "Let's get away from the Israelites! The LORD is fighting for them against Egypt." Then the LORD said to Moses, "Stretch out your hand over the sea so that the waters may flow back over the Egyptians and their chariots and horsemen." Moses stretched out his hand over the sea, and at daybreak the sea went back to its place. The Egyptians were fleeing toward it, and the LORD swept them into the sea. The water flowed back and covered the chariots and horsemen—the entire army of Pharaoh that had followed the Israelites into the sea. Not one of them survived.

Exodus 14:13–14, 21–28

In Egypt

God told Moses and Aaron to get ready for a night the children of Israel would never forget. "I will pass through Egypt about midnight," God said. "The oldest child in every Egyptian family will die. This is My judgment on their sins. I will show all their gods to be false gods. I am the LORD God. Every household of the Israelites shall kill a lamb and spread the blood on the doorposts and lintel of the home where they eat the feast. "

God explained His plans. "The blood on the doorposts will be a sign. When I see the blood, I will pass over the house. The oldest child in your family will not die. I will pass over your families, and you will be safe."

The Israelites ate the meat of the lamb at a special meal that night. Since they were getting ready to leave Egypt, they ate standing up. They were in a hurry to get away from Pharaoh. They wore their traveling clothes and sandals. In one hand they held a staff, while they ate with the other.

At midnight, God's angel of death passed through the land, and many people in Egypt died. Pharaoh's oldest child, as well as the oldest child in all the Egyptian families, died. Even the firstborn of the cattle died. This was God's judgment on the people of Egypt.

In an act of great mercy, God's angel passed over the homes of the Israelites, saving them from death. The Israelites would always remember this deliverance when they celebrated the Passover. They would tell their children what God had done to save them.

God protected His people through the blood of the Passover lamb. The blood was God's sign to the people. When they saw that the angel passed over the homes where blood had been painted on the doorposts, they knew that God was faithful to His covenant with them. They would not be destroyed in Egypt. God had forgiven their sin.

God acted for His people! He saved Israel from Pharaoh's cruel treatment. He blessed them with the Passover meal. Now He was showing His power and love by providing Moses to lead His people out of Egypt.

Out of Egypt

1. How did *God lead His people by day? by night?*

_____

_____

_____

2. Describe *the Egyptian army.*

_____

_____

_____

3. Describe *the Israelites' reaction to the Egyptian army.*

_____

_____

_____

4. How did *Moses encourage God's people?*

_____

_____

_____

5. What do you *think is miraculous about events at the Red Sea?*

_____

_____

Free!

God's rescue at the Red Sea was the greatest act of deliverance for His Old Testament people. God proved to them that He was a faithful Father. In response to God's provision of a dry path through the Red Sea, the people offered praises to God for His mercy.

In Baptism, God rescues His New Testament people. The crossing of the Red Sea is a picture, or type, of God's grace to us in Baptism. Jesus is the Lamb of God, and through His death and resurrection, we pass through sin and death and receive forgiveness and eternal life. In Christ, we are safe from all our enemies.

• **What problems do you face in life?**

• **How has God rescued you?**

• **How did God use water in His rescue?**

• **What is miraculous about your rescue?**

My Song of Praise

• **The Israelites sang to the Lord to praise Him for rescuing them (Exodus 15). In the song, they praised God for who He is and what He had done for them. Read this song. Then take time to write your own song of praise to God.**

I will sing to the Lord, for He is highly exalted.

The Lord is . . .

The Lord has . . .

By His mighty power He has . . .

I will praise Him for . . .

Sign: _____

Date: _____

With My Family

• **Ask your family** to commemorate your deliverance from the slavery of sin by celebrating your Baptism birthday this year. If you have not been baptized, ask your family to talk with your teacher and pastor about the possibility of being baptized.

• **Ask any family** members who were present at your Baptism to share their memories of that day.

With My Mentor

• **Read Exodus** 15 with your mentor. Ask your mentor to share a favorite hymn or praise song and tell why it is special.

• **Ask your mentor** to join you in some small act of service as a way to express your gratitude for God's lifesaving rescue. Your mentor may be able to help you think of ideas. If possible, do this service anonymously.

God Leads His People to the Promised Land

Joshua told the people, "Consecrate yourselves, for tomorrow the LORD will do amazing things among you." Joshua said to the priests, "Take up the ark of the covenant and pass on ahead of the people." So they took it up and went ahead of them. And the LORD said to Joshua, "Today I will begin to exalt you in the eyes of all Israel, so they may know that I am with you as I was with Moses." . . .

So when the people broke camp to cross the Jordan, the priests carrying the ark of the covenant went ahead of them. Now the Jordan is at flood stage all during harvest. Yet as soon as the priests who carried the ark reached the Jordan and their feet touched the water's edge, the water from upstream stopped flowing. It piled up in a heap a great distance away, at a town called Adam in the vicinity of Zarethan, while the water flowing down to the Sea of the Arabah (the Salt Sea) was completely cut off. So the people crossed over opposite Jericho. The priests who carried the ark of the covenant of the LORD stood firm on dry ground in the middle of the Jordan, while all Israel passed by until the whole nation had completed the crossing on dry ground.

Joshua 3:5–7, 14–17

The Ninth Commandment

You shall not covet your neighbor's house.

What does this mean? We should fear and love God so that we do not scheme to get our neighbor's inheritance or house, or get it in a way which only appears right, but help and be of service to him in keeping it.

The Tenth Commandment

You shall not covet your neighbor's wife, or his manservant or maidservant, his ox or donkey, or anything that belongs to your neighbor.

What does this mean? We should fear and love God so that we do not entice or force away our neighbor's wife, workers, or animals, or turn them against him, but urge them to stay and do their duty.

All the Comforts of Home

Have you ever had to be away from home for a long time? Perhaps you went away to camp for a summer or spent a few weeks with relatives in another city. Maybe your entire family accompanied a parent who worked on a special assignment for a while.

- **What did you miss about your home?**

- **What did you plan to do when you returned home?**

What I Missed Most	What I Would Do If I Were Home

God Provides a New Leader

For forty years, Moses led the Israelites through the desert on their way to the land of Canaan. As consequences of previous sins, God would not let Moses or his brother, Aaron, enter the Promised Land. After a brief glimpse into Canaan, Moses died, and God buried him on Mount Nebo.

God commissioned Moses' aide Joshua to lead the people into the Promised Land. God made a remarkable promise to Joshua: "As I was with Moses, so I will be with you; I will never leave you nor forsake you. Be strong and courageous, because you will lead these people to inherit the land I swore to their forefathers to give them" (Joshua 1:5–6).

1. **If you were Joshua**, what fears would you have had about the future?

_____

_____

_____

_____

2. **What assurance** would you have received from God?

_____

_____

_____

_____

Across the Jordan

God kept His promise to Israel. He brought His chosen people out of slavery in Egypt into "a good and spacious land, a land flowing with milk and honey" (Exodus 3:8).

When they arrived at the Jordan River, the Israelites' journey was not yet complete. God was calling His people to take possession of the land. They were to settle down, build houses, plant gardens, and raise families. Each step of the way, Israel faced problems.

As God commanded, Joshua led Israel's armies against the people living throughout the land God had promised to give His people. As they conquered the cities, they destroyed the temples and the idols of the Canaanite people who lived and worshiped in the land.

After conquering the land, Joshua divided it among the twelve tribes of Israel. The Levites, who did not receive a tribal territory because they were responsible for the tabernacle, were given towns in which to live.

God gave the Israelites victory over all their enemies in the land of Canaan. He gave them the land He had promised to their ancestors. As they settled in their homeland, God gave them rest from their years of wandering and warfare. Before he died, Joshua blessed the Israelites and made a covenant for them with God. Joshua wanted God's people to live holy lives and to find contentment in the land God had given them.

Achan's Fall Begins with Coveting

Once during the time of war against Israel's enemies, God revealed to Joshua that a sin had been committed among the people. Items that had been devoted to God had been stolen and lies had been told. God directed Joshua to a man named Achan. "Tell me what you have done," Joshua said.

Achan replied, "It is true! I have sinned against the LORD, the God of Israel. When I saw in the plunder a beautiful robe from Babylonia, all the silver, and all the gold, I coveted them and took them and hid them in my tent."

After the stolen items were retrieved, all of Israel assembled and stoned Achan to death as punishment for his crime. (Joshua 7:10–25).

- **What is coveting?**

- **Explain how the following words from the Book of James are illustrated in the account of Achan: "Each one is tempted when, by his own evil desire, he is dragged away and enticed. Then, after desire has conceived, it gives birth to sin; and sin, when it is full-grown, gives birth to death" (James 1:14–15).**

- **Review the Ninth and Tenth Commandments. What example of coveting and its effects can you provide from our world?**

- **Explain these words of Paul to Timothy: "Godliness with contentment is great gain" (1 Timothy 6:6).**

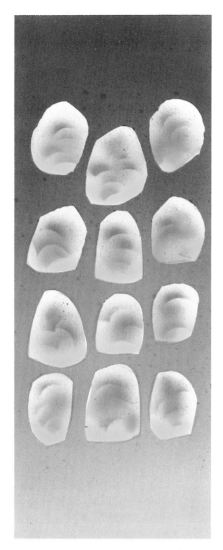

And Joshua set up at Gilgal the twelve stones they had taken out of the Jordan. He said to the Israelites, "In the future when your descendants ask their fathers, 'What do these stones mean?' tell them, 'Israel crossed the Jordan on dry ground.' For the LORD your God dried up the Jordan before you until you had crossed over. The LORD your God did to the Jordan just what He had done to the Red Sea when He dried it up before us until we had crossed over. He did this so that all the peoples of the earth might know that the hand of the LORD is powerful and so that you might always fear the LORD your God."

Joshua 4:20–24

Homeward Bound

In Hebrew, Joshua means "the Lord saves." Joshua served as a picture of another Savior whom God would send to His people. Like the Israelites, all of us wander endlessly in the desert of sin, unable to go home to our heavenly Father. The Law cannot take us home to heaven because no human being can obey it perfectly. So God sent His Son, Jesus, as a human being to obey the Law for us and to die on the cross, receiving the punishment we deserve for our sin. Jesus also defeated our worst enemies—sin, death, and the power of the devil. God the Holy Spirit gives us faith to believe in Jesus as our Savior and leads us to follow Him safely to our heavenly home.

God sent Joshua to lead the Israelites into the P_____ L_____.

The Father sends His Son to lead His people to f_____, l_____, and s_____.

God led the Israelites through the J_____ R_____ and set His people apart to serve Him in holiness and c_____.

God declared Jesus to be His beloved Son at His Baptism in the J_____ R_____ and sent Him forth on His mission to provide salvation for all people.

God gave the Israelites a great victory over their e_____.

Christ wins—and gives to us—the victory over s_____, d_____, and the d_____.

God gave the Israelites r_____ from their journey and battles.

Jesus promises us eternal r_____ in h_____.

God saved, journeyed with, and brought His people to the Promised Land. The Israelites trusted God and declared their commitment to their Savior: "We too will serve the LORD, because He is our God" (Joshua 24:18).

- **Because God has saved me through His Son, Jesus, I trust Him and say**

_____

_____

_____

_____

_____

_____

_____

_____

Sign: _____

Date: _____

 **With My Family**

- **Joshua included** his family in his public commitment to God. Read Joshua 24:15 together. Make a list of ways in which you can serve God together with your family. Then thank God for giving you those individuals in your family with whom you can share and live your faith.

- **In what ways** is your family influenced by advertising and media? How do you usually respond to these advertisements? Together thank God for the blessings He has given your family. Ask Him to help you be content with the riches He has given you.

With My Mentor

- **Ask your mentor** to tell you about a time he or she felt especially aware of God's presence when facing the sin of coveting.

- **Jesus, our Savior,** leads us to an eternal home in heaven at the end of our earthly life. Discuss with your mentor how this belief helps us face the death of loved ones or our own death.

In the days when the judges ruled, there was a famine in the land, and a man from Bethlehem in Judah, together with his wife and two sons, went to live for a while in the country of Moab. The man's name was Elimelech, his wife's name Naomi, and the names of his two sons were Mahlon and Kilion. They were Ephrathites from Bethlehem, Judah. And they went to Moab and lived there. Now Elimelech, Naomi's husband, died, and she was left with her two sons. They married Moabite women, one named Orpah and the other Ruth. After they had lived there about ten years, both Mahlon and Kilion also died, and Naomi was left without her two sons and her husband.

But Naomi said, "Return home, my daughters. Why would you come with me? Am I going to have any more sons, who could become your husbands? Return home, my daughters; I am too old to have another husband. Even if I thought there was still hope for me—even if I had a husband tonight and then gave birth to sons—would you wait until they grew up? Would you remain unmarried for them? No, my daughters. It is more bitter for me than for you, because the LORD's hand has gone out against me!" At this they wept again. Then Orpah kissed her mother-in-law good-by, but Ruth clung to her. "Look," said Naomi, "your sister-in-law is going back to her people and her gods. Go back with her." But Ruth replied, "Don't urge me to leave you or to turn back from you. Where you go I will go, and where you stay I will stay. Your people will be my people and your God my God."

Ruth 1:1–5, 11–16

God Brings Ruth into His Family

The Fourth Commandment

Honor your father and your mother.

What does this mean? We should fear and love God so that we do not despise or anger our parents and other authorities, but honor them, serve and obey them, love and cherish them.

The Close of the Commandments

What does God say about all these commandments? He says: "I, the Lord your God, am a jealous God, punishing the children for the sin of the fathers to the third and fourth generation of those who hate Me, but showing love to a thousand generations of those who love Me and keep My commandments." [Ex. 20:5–6]

What does this mean? God threatens to punish all who break these commandments. Therefore, we should fear His wrath and not do anything against them. But He promises grace and every blessing to all who keep these commandments. Therefore, we should also love and trust in Him and gladly do what He commands.

Ready to Go?

"It's got to be a family decision," says Dad. But you know he really wants to take the promotion. The only downside is that it will require moving to another state. Dad sits in front of you, asking what you think your family should do. It will mean leaving behind your friends, your neighborhood, and your team. What would you say if you were in this situation?

Two for the Road

After Joshua died, Israel gradually forgot about God. The people forgot all that the Lord had done for them. He had freed them from slavery in Egypt and given them their own land. The people turned to worshiping Baal. God was angry at their idolatry. He punished them by letting their neighbors overpower them.

When Israel cried out to God for relief, He helped them. He was still their covenant Lord; He would not forget His promises, even though the people sinned and forgot their promises. God's mercy prompted Him to choose individuals to be "saviors" or "judges" of Israel. Each judge ruled the people only until the enemy had been conquered. Each judge was a direct spokesman of the Lord to Israel. Besides Gideon and Samuel, some of the better known judges were Deborah and Samson.

The story of Naomi and Ruth takes place in "the days when the judges ruled" (Ruth 1:1). Though Naomi and her family lived in Moab, God was still faithful to His covenant with Israel, His people.

1. **What hardships** *did Naomi face in Moab?*

   _____
   _____
   _____

2. **What hardships** *did Ruth face in Moab?*

   _____
   _____
   _____

3. **Do you think** *adversity usually brings family members closer together, or does adversity usually pull family members further apart? Explain.*

   _____
   _____
   _____

4. **Describe the** *relationship between Naomi and Ruth.*

   _____
   _____
   _____

My Kinsman-Redeemer

When God protected and blessed Ruth, He showed His faithfulness to those who love and trust in Him. Because Ruth loved God, she served and honored her mother-in-law as God commands in the Fourth Commandment. God blessed Ruth with a new husband, gave them a child, and from this child many prominent descendants, including the kings of Israel and, finally, the Savior of the world. Boaz was Ruth's kinsman-redeemer, but the ultimate Redeemer is Christ Jesus. He came to redeem us from sin.

Ruth and Boaz remind us that God is faithful to His Word. He fulfilled His promise to send the Savior, Jesus. By His life, death, and resurrection, Jesus makes us His children, free from the power of sin, death, and the devil.

- **How did Boaz arrange to marry Ruth?**

  _____

- **How did Boaz demonstrate his commitment to Ruth?**

  _____

- **What does it mean to be a redeemer?**

  _____

  _____

My God and My Parents

I know that Jesus, my Redeemer, is always with my family and me. I was especially thankful for His love and care when . . .

_____

_____

_____

_____

_____

_____

Sign: _____

Date: _____

Talk about it — With My Family

- **Think of some** small acts of kindness you can do for family members. Identify and carry out an activity that can encourage a family member in their Christian faith.

- **Talk to older** family members—grandparents and great-grandparents—about customs they remember. What was their family life like? What was school life like? What special customs do they remember? Identify family customs that encouraged people in their Christian faith.

With My Mentor

- **Share with your mentor** those things about your parents and grandparents for which you are especially thankful to God.

- **Discuss with your mentor** times when listening to the advice of others has been very helpful. Ask your mentor's input on something that is troubling you.

God Promises David a Kingdom

The Fourth Petition

Give us this day our daily bread.

What does this mean? God certainly gives daily bread to everyone without our prayers, even to all evil people, but we pray in this petition that God would lead us to realize this and to receive our daily bread with thanksgiving.

What is meant by daily bread? Daily bread includes everything that has to do with the support and needs of the body, such as food, drink, clothing, shoes, house, home, land, animals, money, goods, a devout husband or wife, devout children, devout workers, devout and faithful rulers, good government, good weather, peace, health, self-control, good reputation, good friends, faithful neighbors, and the like.

A Leader for the People

Four long black limousines pull up in front of your school. A dozen distinguished-looking government officials climb out and walk quickly through the front doors. Their mission? To speak with each member of your class.

You file down to the cafeteria, where the tables are ready with a stack of tests for you to take. After the testing, you are asked strange questions in a lengthy interview. When you return to your class, your friends are asking, "For whom are they looking? Who will be selected?" Naturally, you think about Michael, the tallest and fastest guy in your school. Or Roni, the smartest girl in all your classes.

That night the word of the LORD came to Nathan, saying:

"Now then, tell My servant David, 'This is what the LORD Almighty says: I took you from the pasture and from following the flock to be ruler over My people Israel. I have been with you wherever you have gone, and I have cut off all your enemies from before you. Now I will make your name great, like the names of the greatest men of the earth. And I will provide a place for My people Israel and will plant them so that they can have a home of their own and no longer be disturbed. . . .

'The LORD declares to you that the LORD Himself will establish a house for you: When your days are over and you rest with your fathers, I will raise up your offspring to succeed you, who will come from your own body, and I will establish his kingdom. He is the one who will build a house for My Name, and I will establish the throne of his kingdom forever. I will be his father, and he will be My son. . . . Your house and your kingdom will endure forever before Me; your throne will be established forever.' "

2 Samuel 7:4, 8–10, 11b–14, 16

41

At the end of the day, the whole school assembles in the gym. The leader of the government agency says, "We're here looking for just the right person, the one who will become the leader of our nation. This person's family will be leaders for generations to come. We have made our selection, and our new leader is . . . *you!*"

• **Describe your feelings.**

God Looks at the Heart

One day God sent the prophet Samuel to Bethlehem to the house of Jesse. God had chosen one of Jesse's sons to be the king of Israel. Samuel was to anoint the new king. This would be an exciting event, for Jesse had many sons. Samuel did not know which son the Lord had chosen.

"I wish to see each of your sons," Samuel told Jesse. So the oldest son stepped forward. He was strong and handsome. Samuel thought, This must be the Lord's choice. But the Lord said, "Do not look on the outward appearance. I look at the heart."

Then Jesse had his other sons walk before Samuel. Each time the Lord told Samuel, "I have not chosen this one." So Samuel announced, "The Lord has not chosen any of these seven sons. Are all your sons here?"

"The youngest is out in the fields tending the sheep."

"Send for him," directed Samuel. The boy came when he was called. His name was David. Samuel saw that he was a handsome young man too.

"Anoint him," said the Lord. "This is the new king."

Samuel took a horn of oil and poured it over David's head right before his father and his brothers. God's Spirit came upon David from this time on. God had mighty things for David to do.

Blessings of the Kingdom

The Spirit of the Lord made David a great and mighty king.

During David's reign, Israel became a great nation. He fought and won many battles against Israel's enemies.

David's house would last forever because the Son of God would be born of his descendants. Jesus is the Anointed One of God, the Christ, who completed the plan of salvation for all sinners. Through His work, God keeps His covenant of life with us.

The story of King David shows how God keeps His promises to His people. God made David great by sending His Son, Jesus, into this world as a member of David's family. We praise God when we confess that Jesus Christ is our Lord and King.

Our King rules us by His grace and love. Because He is a merciful God, He calls us into His kingdom. God gives us His Holy Spirit so that we believe that we are in the kingdom of His Son. God's Spirit helps us live as His chosen people.

- **How can I express my thanks to God for the gift of life?**

_____

_____

_____

- **How can I praise God for His daily protection?**

_____

_____

_____

- **How can I serve God as I live with my family?**

_____

_____

_____

Sign: _____

Date: _____

Talk about it *With My Family*

- **Each day this week,** help your family take time to discuss one of the blessings God has given your family. As part of your discussion, volunteer to read the Fourth Petition of the Lord's Prayer and Martin Luther's explanation of it.

- **Ask your family,** "What things do we do that show others that we are loyal subjects of our King, Jesus Christ?" List ways that your citizenship in God's kingdom is evident in your actions.

With My Mentor

- **Share with your mentor** what you've learned about having Jesus as your King. Reflect together on what it means to be a part of a royal family.

- **Read together the** Fourth Petition and its explanation. Ask what gifts or abilities your mentor has been given by God. How does she or he use these gifts in service to the King? Explore together what special gifts and blessings you have been given.

God Blesses Solomon

Then the king and all Israel with him offered sacrifices before the LORD. Solomon offered a sacrifice of fellowship offerings to the LORD: twenty-two thousand cattle and a hundred and twenty thousand sheep and goats. So the king and all the Israelites dedicated the temple of the LORD. On that same day the king consecrated the middle part of the courtyard in front of the temple of the LORD, and there he offered burnt offerings, grain offerings and the fat of the fellowship offerings, because the bronze altar before the LORD was too small to hold the burnt offerings, the grain offerings and the fat of the fellowship offerings. So Solomon observed the festival at that time, and all Israel with him—a vast assembly, people from Lebo Hamath to the Wadi of Egypt. They celebrated it before the LORD our God for seven days and seven days more, fourteen days in all. On the following day he sent the people away. They blessed the king and then went home, joyful and glad in heart for all the good things the LORD had done for His servant David and His people Israel.

1 Kings 8:62–66

The Third Commandment

Remember the Sabbath day by keeping it holy.

What does this mean? We should fear and love God so that we do not despise preaching and His Word, but hold it sacred and gladly hear and learn it.

A Place for Me

What's your favorite place?

"It depends," you say. At different times of the day you prefer to be at different places. Each place you go is important. Each place is unique. All the places you go to during a day enrich your life.

My favorite place when I am

hungry _____

_____

energized _____

_____

sad _____

_____

frustrated or hurt_____

_____

doing homework _____

_____

bored _____

_____

A House for God

David was a man of war. His son Solomon was a man of peace. David wished to build a temple for God's glory, but God had said that Solomon should build the temple while the nation was at peace.

Solomon made an agreement with Hiram, king of Tyre. "I am going to build a house for the name of the Lord my God," he said. "I want to have cedars from Lebanon in this house. Will you cut them down for me? None of us can cut timber like your people can."

Hiram agreed. His people made rafts out of the logs they cut. They floated them down the seacoast. Solomon paid for the work with wheat and oil. Solomon also used skilled artists, builders, and workers to complete the temple in Jerusalem.

Finally, after seven years, the temple was finished. Solomon called all the people together to dedicate it.

The priests carried the ark of the covenant into the temple. They put all the holy vessels in their proper places. When the priests came out of the temple, they could not continue their service because a cloud filled the temple. The glory of the Lord filled the house of the Lord. Solomon said, "Praise be to the LORD, the God of Israel, who with His own hand has fulfilled what He promised with His own mouth to my father David" (1 Kings 8:15).

1. **Why did Solomon** *want to build a temple for the Lord?*

   _____

   _____

   _____

2. **How did the people** *of Israel help to build the temple?*

   _____

   _____

   _____

3. **How would you** *describe the dedication of the temple?*

   _____

   _____

   _____

4. **How do** *people keep the Sabbath Day holy?*

   _____

   _____

   _____

The Glory of God

God's glory filled the temple.

God was present with His people. Years before, God promised David that his son would build a temple and sit on his throne. God's promise to David and Solomon pointed forward to the Son of David, Jesus Christ. The covenant with David and the people of Israel was fulfilled when Jesus lived, died, and rose again. Through Jesus, God confirmed His covenant to save His people.

God's highest glory is in His Son, who came so that we might live with God forever. God has given us the high privilege of knowing Jesus as our risen and living Savior. He is with us every day. He lives in us.

God comes to us through His Word and Sacraments. Through faith we understand the covenant He made with us in Baptism. He is our faithful God! When, by God's grace, we listen to His Word, believe it, and live according to it, we honor God in the ways He has described in the Third Commandment. God blesses us in Christ!

- **When I listen to God's Word of love and forgiveness in Christ, God . . .**

_____

_____

_____

_____

_____

Sign: _____

Date: _____

 **With My Family**

- **With a parent,** grandparent, or other older family member, complete the following sentence: "I feel I have been blessed by God with the gift(s) of . . ." Discuss your gifts together, and thank God for His mercy and goodness in Jesus.

- **Visit your church** and take photographs of the exterior, the sanctuary, and your family and fellow believers. As you show your pictures, talk about the blessings of keeping the Sabbath Day holy.

With My Mentor

- **Share with each other** a gift that you have received from God. Share a goal or way in which you plan to use your gift to God's glory in the weeks or months ahead.

- **Write a short note** to your mentor, reflecting on the ideas in last weekend's sermon or worship theme as they relate to you.

13

God Empowers Elijah

The Introduction to the Lord's Prayer

Our Father who art in heaven.

What does this mean? With these words God tenderly invites us to believe that He is our true Father and that we are His true children, so that with all boldness and confidence we may ask Him as dear children ask their dear father.

The First Petition

Hallowed be Thy name.

What does this mean? God's name is certainly holy in itself, but we pray in this petition that it may be kept holy among us also.

How is God's name kept holy? God's name is kept holy when the Word of God is taught in its truth and purity, and we, as the children of God, also lead holy lives according to it. Help us to do this, dear Father in heaven! But anyone who teaches or lives contrary to God's Word profanes the name of God among us. Protect us from this, heavenly Father!

The First Commandment

You shall have no other gods.

What does this mean? We should fear, love, and trust in God above all things.

Then Elijah said to all the people, "Come here to me." They came to him, and he repaired the altar of the LORD, which was in ruins. Elijah took twelve stones, one for each of the tribes descended from Jacob, to whom the word of the LORD had come, saying, "Your name shall be Israel." With the stones he built an altar in the name of the LORD, and he dug a trench around it large enough to hold two seahs of seed. He arranged the wood, cut the bull into pieces and laid it on the wood. Then he said to them, "Fill four large jars with water and pour it on the offering and on the wood." "Do it again," he said, and they did it again. "Do it a third time," he ordered, and they did it the third time. The water ran down around the altar and even filled the trench. At the time of sacrifice, the prophet Elijah stepped forward and prayed: "O LORD, God of Abraham, Isaac and Israel, let it be known today that You are God in Israel and that I am Your servant and have done all these things at Your command. Answer me, O LORD, answer me, so these people will know that You, O LORD, are God, and that You are turning their hearts back again." Then the fire of the LORD fell and burned up the sacrifice, the wood, the stones and the soil, and also licked up the water in the trench. When all the people saw this, they fell prostrate and cried, "The LORD—He is God! The LORD—He is God!"

1 Kings 18:30–39

A Friendly Contest

Most people like contests. It's fun to compete against friends for first prize in your class. It's also fun to compete against other teams on the sports field or in the gym.

Even friendly contests can be frightening.

What if I can't finish? What if I lose? What will people think of me? _____

_____

Contests I Might Win _____

_____

Contests I Might Lose _____

_____

Contests I Want to Win _____

_____

The Contest

When God made His covenant with Israel, He said, "I am the LORD your God. You shall have no other gods before Me."

For a while, God's people worshiped and obeyed the Lord. Soon, however, they began worshiping other gods, like the golden calf. Soon after the dedication of the temple, Solomon, too, forgot the Lord. He began to worship the gods of his foreign wives. Worship of the Lord God of Israel was neglected and soon forgotten. Solomon led his people to turn away from the Lord. God punished Israel, and the kingdom was divided.

Yet God remembered His promise to David and His people. He wanted His people to repent and trust Him. God sent brave and faithful men—His prophets—to speak His Word.

God sent the prophet Elijah to tell King Ahab that a drought would wither the country of Israel. Ahab was very angry with Elijah. Ahab tried to kill him.

Then Elijah went away for three years. When Ahab saw him again, he greeted him, "Is it you, you troublemaker for Israel?" The drought had been devastating.

Elijah defended himself. "I have not troubled Israel," he retorted, "you have! You have not obeyed God's commandments. You pray to the false god Baal."

Then Elijah called all the people of Israel to Mount Carmel. He proclaimed God's Word to them. "You are at the fork in the road. It is time for you to choose which way you will go. How long can you go without making up your mind? If the Lord is God, follow Him. If Baal is God, follow him."

What did the people answer Elijah? Not a word.

Showdown

God gave His prophets knowledge of His will. By the power of His Spirit, He gave them special messages and the courage to proclaim these messages to His people. When God's people began to worship false gods, these prophets preached God's judgment on idolatry and sin. They worked to keep Israel faithful to the true God. They reminded the people of God's covenant of grace and mercy to forgive their sins.

A number of God's prophets wrote their messages. These are preserved as books of the Bible in the Old Testament. Habakkuk, Hosea, Isaiah, and Jeremiah are some of these prophets. Their books are the Word of God for us also today.

1. **Why is Elijah** *concerned for the people of Israel according to the First Commandment?*

   _____
   _____
   _____

2. **What does Elijah** *want to demonstrate by the contest on Mount Carmel?*

   _____
   _____
   _____

3. **What words** *describe Elijah's thoughts and feelings about the contest?*

   _____
   _____
   _____

God's Word Today

God is great! He is the only true God. He is angry when people give Him a low priority in their lives. Have we ever done this by loving a person or an activity more than God? Have we done this by disobeying His commands? Have we done this by living contrary to God's Word?

When we sin, Jesus speaks His Word of forgiveness and life to us. He is our Prophet, Priest, and King, who saves us through His death and resurrection.

God sends His prophets into our life too. Pastors and teachers preach and teach God's Word. When they teach God's Word in its truth and purity, they are helping us "lead holy lives according to it," as the explanation of the First Petition says. Jesus lives in us through our Baptism. Praise be the name of our God!

- **In response to our heavenly Father's invitation to come to Him in prayer (Matthew 7:7–8), write a prayer based on Psalm 113 thanking Him for His Word and His salvation in Christ!**

_____

_____

_____

_____

_____

_____

_____

_____

Sign: _____

Date: _____

Talk about it · With My Family

- **Share with** your family a memory of God's mercy and power in your lives. In a prayer thank Him for His incredible love and goodness.

- **Discuss the** idolatry you see in our world today. In what ways do people put other objects before God? During your family devotions, ask God to forgive you and your family for placing other things ahead of God in your lives. Ask for His strength to serve Him faithfully.

With My Mentor

- **Together visit** a widow or widower in your congregation. Bring a small gift of flowers or baked goods. Share encouraging words from Scripture or a prayer. Talk about how God is our loving Father who cares for us. Pray the Lord's Prayer together.

- **Read together** several other great stories involving Elijah found in 1 Kings 21 and 2 Kings 2. Discuss how Elijah hallowed God's name throughout his life. List several ways each of you hallow God's name in your own lives.

God Preserves His People through Esther

The Eighth Commandment

You shall not give false testimony against your neighbor.

What does this mean? We should fear and love God so that we do not tell lies about our neighbor, betray him, slander him, or hurt his reputation, but defend him, speak well of him, and explain everything in the kindest way.

Big Trouble

Julie knew she would regret her words even as they were leaving her mouth. Spoken in anger, her words were sure to cost her a friendship—maybe more than one. Instead of saying something to help to heal the damage that had been done, she had made things worse. What should I do now? she wondered.

1. **When have you** *found yourself in a situation like that described above?*

   _____

   _____

2. **What would you** *do if you were Julie?*

   _____

   _____

3. **"Words can hurt** *and words can kill." Give an example of each way words can be used.*

   _____

   _____

So the king and Haman went to dine with Queen Esther, and as they were drinking wine on that second day, the king again asked, "Queen Esther, what is your petition? It will be given you. What is your request? Even up to half the kingdom, it will be granted." Then Queen Esther answered, "If I have found favor with you, O king, and if it pleases your majesty, grant me my life—this is my petition. And spare my people—this is my request. For I and my people have been sold for destruction and slaughter and annihilation. If we had merely been sold as male and female slaves, I would have kept quiet, because no such distress would justify disturbing the king." King Xerxes asked Queen Esther, "Who is he? Where is the man who has dared to do such a thing?" Esther said, "The adversary and enemy is this vile Haman." Then Haman was terrified before the king and queen. The king got up in a rage, left his wine and went out into the palace garden. But Haman, real-

Continued on page 52

God had to destroy a city to save His faithless people.

The people of Israel were trusting in idols to protect them instead of trusting in God. They were wrong in their hopes. God sent prophets to tell the people how wrong they were. He sent Jeremiah to Jerusalem and Ezekiel to captives in Babylon.

"Maybe they will listen," God said to His prophets. "Maybe each one will turn from his evil ways. Then I will not punish them for their evil."

God gave His prophets a special announcement for the people: "Listen to Me. Walk in the way I have given you. Pay attention to the words of My prophets. If you don't, I will destroy the temple. I will make Jerusalem a city that all the nations despise. It will be ruined."

The people of Israel did not like this announcement. They did not listen to God's warning against their false worship and evil ways. God used Babylon to accomplish His purposes.

King Nebuchadnezzar of Babylon sent his army against Jerusalem. The warriors surrounded the city and battered the walls. At last they broke through. They set fire to the king's palace. They even destroyed the temple and tore down the city walls. They took the people captive and led them away to Babylon as slaves.

- **How would you describe the captivity and exile that the people of Israel experienced (Ezekiel 7)?**

_____

_____

_____

_____

Continued from page 51
izing that the king had already decided his fate, stayed behind to beg Queen Esther for his life. Just as the king returned from the palace garden to the banquet hall, Haman was falling on the couch where Esther was reclining. The king exclaimed, "Will he even molest the queen while she is with me in the house?" As soon as the word left the king's mouth, they covered Haman's face. Then Harbona, one of the eunuchs attending the king, said, "A gallows seventy-five feet high stands by Haman's house. He had it made for Mordecai, who spoke up to help the king." The king said, "Hang him on it!" So they hanged Haman on the gallows he had prepared for Mordecai. Then the king's fury subsided.

Esther 7

The Savior God

The Book of Esther is filled with suspense, romance, action, intrigue, and a happy ending. Yet, surprisingly, the story never mentions God! King Ahasuerus, Esther, Mordecai, and Haman are the people who make plans, carry out decisions, and wait for events to happen. In truth, God is at work in the story. The God who used the Persians to free His people after a long exile (539 BC) was working behind the scenes to preserve the house of Israel. Through Esther, God showed His mercy and blessed His people. Through Jesus, God saves and blesses us today.

- **God empowered Esther to speak up for other. What opportunities do you have to speak up for others?**

_____

_____

_____

_____

_____

_____

Sign: _____

Date: _____

Talk about it — With My Family

- **Hamantaschen** are triangular shaped cookies or pastries with a variety of fillings (jellies, cream cheese, and fruit). They are eaten during the Jewish holiday *Purim* and are said to remind one of Haman's triangular hat or ears. Share hamantaschen with your family. Discuss the significance of the triangular shape—Father, Son, and Holy Spirit—in the Christian faith.

- **Talk together** with your family members, encouraging each other by telling one another things you especially like or appreciate about one another. Discuss: How does this activity relate to the Eighth Commandment?

With My Mentor

- **Talk about** the importance of "explain[ing] everything in the kindest way."

- **How did God** prepare Esther for her future? Discuss with your mentor ways in which he or she feels that God has directed his or her life. How might God be preparing you for your future?

God Restores His People

In the first year of Cyrus king of Persia, in order to fulfill the word of the LORD spoken by Jeremiah, the LORD moved the heart of Cyrus king of Persia to make a proclamation throughout his realm and to put it in writing:

"This is what Cyrus king of Persia says:

'The LORD, the God of heaven, has given me all the kingdoms of the earth and He has appointed me to build a temple for Him at Jerusalem in Judah. Anyone of His people among you—may his God be with him, and let him go up to Jerusalem in Judah and build the temple of the LORD, the God of Israel, the God who is in Jerusalem. And the people of any place where survivors may now be living are to provide him with silver and gold, with goods and livestock, and with freewill offerings for the temple of God in Jerusalem.' "

. . . When the seventh month came and the Israelites had settled in their towns, the people assembled as one man in Jerusalem. Then Jeshua son of Jozadak and his fellow priests and Zerubbabel son of Shealtiel and his associates began to build the altar of the God of Israel to sacrifice burnt offerings on it, in accordance with what is written in the Law of Moses the man of God. Despite their fear of the peoples around them, they built the altar on its foundation and sacrificed burnt offerings on it to the LORD, both the morning and evening sacrifices.

Ezra 1:1–4; 3:1–3

Luther's Morning and Evening Prayers

Morning Prayer

I thank You, my heavenly Father, through Jesus Christ, Your dear Son, that You have kept me this night from all harm and danger; and I pray that You would keep me this day also from sin and every evil, that all my doings and life may please You. For into Your hands I commend myself, my body and soul, and all things. Let Your holy angel be with me, that the evil foe may have no power over me. Amen.

Evening Prayer

I thank You, my heavenly Father, through Jesus Christ, Your dear Son, that You have graciously kept me this day; and I pray that You would forgive me all my sins where I have done wrong, and graciously keep me this night. For into Your hands I commend myself, my body and soul, and all things. Let Your holy angel be with me, that the evil foe may have no power over me. Amen.

Just a Coincidence?

"It's funny," said Bradley as he tied his shoes. "This is the first Sunday we weren't planning to go fishing with Dad, and Mike asked us to go to his church today."

"That's for sure," agreed his twin brother, Bryan. "If we had moved to Detroit like we had planned, we would never have met Mike. The only house Mom and Dad found here was right next to his family. And now he's our best friend."

"Funny, isn't it?" said Bradley. "But stuff like that just happens . . ."

- **Do you think "stuff" just happens? Or is there a plan behind our lives?**

- **Think about events in your life. Do you remember a time when God used people or events to bring you closer to your Savior?**

A Remnant Returns

Nebuchadnezzar, king of Babylon, had destroyed the temple. Jerusalem was a pile of stones and broken dreams. Once, the Israelites had been a great nation. Now they were a poor, scattered people. God had rescued a faithful few. He called them the "remnant of Israel." They escaped His judgment on Israel's idolatry. They trusted God to keep His promise of salvation. Because of God's mercy, they returned to Jerusalem.

Years before they returned, however, God had promised the remnant, "I will make a new covenant with the house of Israel and with the house of Judah." God said,

> "I will put My law in their minds and write it on their hearts. I will be their God, and they will be My people. . . . They will all know Me, from the least of them to the greatest," declares the LORD. "For I will forgive their wickedness and will remember their sins no more." Jeremiah 31:33–34

God had promised His salvation. He had promised to send the Messiah.

1. **How did God** show His mercy . . .

   a. *to His people in exile?*

   b. *through Cyrus?*

   c. *during the trip back to Jerusalem?*

   d. *when His people arrived at Jerusalem?*

   e. *through Christ?*

Restored in Christ

In His mercy, God returned His people to their homeland. He allowed them to rebuild the temple and worship Him. In His mercy, He restored them as His people through His Word. God watched over the remnant He rescued. From this remnant He brought His Son, Jesus, Israel's Messiah and the Savior of the world.

By the blood of Jesus Christ shed on the cross, God returns His people to Himself in mercy. This is the new covenant. God has saved us from our sin and rebellion through Christ. He has restored us as His children. We are His people in Jesus.

As God's people through faith in Jesus, our heavenly Father invites us to come to Him in prayer regularly and often. He invites us to pray and has promised to hear us. He promises to forgive, help, and bless us through Jesus Christ, His Son.

Reflect on God's mercy and His call to serve Jesus.

- **I remember God's goodness to me in**

_____

_____

- **I am thankful to God for**

_____

_____

- **I want to ask God to help me by**

_____

_____

Sign: _____

Date: _____

Talk about it — With My Family

- **God's people** who returned to Jerusalem helped to rebuild the temple. Look for projects at your church that you can tackle as a family. Check with the custodian, board of trustees, maintenance committee, secretarial staff, or pastor for ideas and permission.

- **Before God's** people began working on the temple, they built an altar and worshiped God. Keep worship at the center of your family life, praising God for salvation through Jesus. Pray Luther's Morning Prayer together each morning and Luther's Evening Prayer each night.

With My Mentor

- **Zerubbabel and** Ezra were called by God to the task of leading His people. Ask your mentor to tell you how God led him or her to a specific area of work in the church.

- **Is God calling** you to serve full-time in the church? Discuss professions that might fit your interests and abilities. Pray together that the Holy Spirit would guide you as you choose your vocation in life.

Jesus' Birth

The Second Article

I believe . . . in Jesus Christ, His only Son, our Lord, who was conceived by the Holy Spirit, born of the Virgin Mary, suffered under Pontius Pilate, was crucified, died and was buried. He descended into hell. The third day He rose again from the dead. He ascended into heaven and sits at the right hand of God, the Father Almighty. From thence He will come to judge the living and the dead.

What does this mean? I believe that Jesus Christ, true God, begotten of the Father from eternity, and also true man, born of the Virgin Mary, is my Lord, who has redeemed me, a lost and condemned person, purchased and won me from all sins, from death, and from the power of the devil; not with gold or silver, but with His holy, precious blood and with His innocent suffering and death, that I may be His own and live under Him in His kingdom and serve Him in everlasting righteousness, innocence, and blessedness, just as He is risen from the dead, lives and reigns to all eternity. This is most certainly true.

Right Time, Right Place

When you study history, you learn dates and locations, when and where events happened, to better understand the importance of the events. Dates and locations have significance. The Revolutionary War, for example, did not happen yesterday, and it did not happen at the North Pole!

And there were shepherds living out in the fields nearby, keeping watch over their flocks at night. An angel of the Lord appeared to them, and the glory of the Lord shone around them, and they were terrified. But the angel said to them, "Do not be afraid. I bring you good news of great joy that will be for all the people. Today in the town of David a Savior has been born to you; He is Christ the Lord. This will be a sign to you: You will find a baby wrapped in cloths and lying in a manger." Suddenly a great company of the heavenly host appeared with the angel, praising God and saying, "Glory to God in the highest, and on earth peace to men on whom His favor rests."

When the angels had left them and gone into heaven, the shepherds said to one another, "Let's go to Bethlehem and see this thing that has happened, which the Lord has told us about."

So they hurried off and found Mary and Joseph, and the baby, who was lying in the manger. When they had seen Him, they spread the word concerning what had been told them about this child, and all who heard it were amazed at what the shepherds said to them. But Mary treasured up all these things and pondered them in her heart. The shepherds returned, glorifying and praising God for all the things they had heard and seen, which were just as they had been told.

Luke 2:8–20

Match the following events with the dates they happened.

The Exodus from Egypt	5 BC	Constantine, Ruler of the Roman Empire
The First Olympic Games in Greece	AD 800	Charlemagne Crowned Emperor
	AD 1492	
Julius Caesar Murdered in Rome	AD 325	Christopher Columbus Sails from Portugal
	AD 1517	
Jesus Born in Bethlehem	776 BC	Ninety-five Theses Written
	44 BC	
	1446 BC	

God Sends His Son

Mary lived in Nazareth, a village nestled in the hills of Galilee. She was engaged to Joseph, a descendant of King David. Mary had grown up hearing the stories of God giving His promises to His people in the Holy Scriptures.

For to us a child is born, to us a son is given, and the government will be on His shoulders. And He will be called Wonderful Counselor, Mighty God, Everlasting Father, Prince of Peace. (Isaiah 9:6)

One day an angel from God came to Mary with remarkable news: it was time for God to fulfill His promises! Mary would have a baby—a son. Yet the child would be no ordinary child: Mary's baby, the angel said, would be God's Son.

When Joseph heard that Mary was to have a baby, he at first thought Mary had been unfaithful to him. Then an angel appeared to Joseph in a dream. Mary's child, the angel said, was conceived by the Holy Spirit. The baby was a boy, and Joseph was to give Him the name *Jesus*, for He would be the Savior of God's people.

Joseph knew that God was keeping the promises He had made to Israel, so he took Mary as his wife.

1. **If you were** *Mary, what would you have written in your journal on the day the angel appeared to you?*

_____

_____

_____

2. **If you were** *Joseph, what would you have written in your journal on the day the angel appeared to you?*

_____

_____

_____

_____

The Right Time

Though spoken centuries before, God fulfilled His promises by giving His Son as a baby to Mary and Joseph. At the right time, God sent His Son into the world. Jesus came to redeem His people from the curse of sin and death.

God kept His promise to send the Messiah—the Savior—through the remnant of Israel. Born into the house of David, the family of Joseph and Mary, Jesus is God in the flesh. His birth is a wonderful mystery. His love for sinful human beings is Good News for all people. Christ is born! Through faith in Jesus, we are God's children, and Jesus is our Brother. Our loving Father adopts us into His family through His Son.

- **God gave the Savior of the world to Mary and Joseph, ordinary people from a quiet, out-of-the-way place. What does it mean to you that God has sent His Son to be your Savior?**

_____

_____

_____

- **Mary and Joseph were probably tired when they arrived in Bethlehem. God provided for their needs. In what ways have you experienced God's love and care when you were tired and alone?**

_____

_____

_____

- **The shepherds were an unlikely group of witnesses to God's gift of His Son. They told everyone about what they saw and heard in Bethlehem. How can you share with others what Jesus has done for you?**

_____

_____

_____

Sign: _____

Date: _____

Talk about it — With My Family

- **Ask your family** to share a Christmas memory. As the sharing takes place, discuss ways your family can focus more on the birth of Jesus during your next Christmas celebration.

- **A bumper sticker** proclaims, "Jesus was homeless too." Sit down with your family and brainstorm ways that you and your family can serve others in need in your community at Christmas. If you aren't sure how to be of service, call your pastor, a local food pantry or homeless shelter, the Salvation Army, or the Red Cross.

With My Mentor

- **Create a Christmas** card for your mentor that includes a Christian Christmas greeting. Be sure to say how much you appreciate your mentor in your faith walk with Jesus.

- **Ask your mentor,** "If you had gone to the manger the first Christmas, what gift would you have brought Jesus?" Explore together what various gifts for Jesus might say about our faith and trust in Him as our Lord and Savior.

Jesus Is Baptized

What Baptism Indicates

What does such baptizing with water indicate? It indicates that the Old Adam in us should by daily contrition and repentance be drowned and die with all sins and evil desires, and that a new man should daily emerge and arise to live before God in righteousness and purity forever.

Where is this written? St. Paul writes in Romans chapter six: "We were therefore buried with Him through baptism into death in order that, just as Christ was raised from the dead through the glory of the Father, we too may live a new life." [Rom. 6:4]

At the River

God in heaven invites us to call Him Father. He loves us so much that despite our sinfulness, He sent Jesus to save us from our sin. He sent His Holy Spirit to strengthen us in faith and

"I baptize you with water for repentance. But after me will come one who is more powerful than I, whose sandals I am not fit to carry. He will baptize you with the Holy Spirit and with fire. His winnowing fork is in His hand, and He will clear His threshing floor, gathering His wheat into the barn and burning up the chaff with unquenchable fire."

Then Jesus came from Galilee to the Jordan to be baptized by John. But John tried to deter Him, saying, "I need to be baptized by You, and do You come to me?"

Jesus replied, "Let it be so now; it is proper for us to do this to fulfill all righteousness." Then John consented.

As soon as Jesus was baptized, He went up out of the water. At that moment heaven was opened, and He saw the Spirit of God descending like a dove and lighting on Him. And a voice from heaven said, "This is My Son, whom I love; with Him I am well pleased."

Matthew 3:11–17

empower us for a new and eternal life in His name. We call our God triune—Father, Son, and Holy Spirit. As John baptized Jesus at the Jordan River, the triune God was present.

God's Son, Savior

To prepare the way for Jesus, God sent John, the son of Zechariah. "Tell the people that the kingdom of God is close at hand," God told John. "Through your message I will turn them to Myself in repentance. Preach to them. Baptize them. Bring them My forgiveness. I will give them faith in Jesus."

Many people gathered to hear John teach. Some thought that he was the Savior. "No," said John, "the Savior is much greater than I am. He is coming very soon."

One day Jesus came to John near the Jordan River. John knew Him right away! But he was surprised when Jesus said, "I am here for you to baptize Me." When His Son was baptized, God announced to the whole world, "Jesus is My Son."

1. **Why was John** *hesitant to baptize Jesus?*

   _____

   _____

   _____

   _____

2. **For what purpose** *did Jesus desire to be baptized?*

   _____

   _____

   _____

   _____

Our Savior God

When God spoke from heaven, He told everyone that Jesus is more than a human being. God proclaimed that Jesus is His own Son—true God with the Father.

God introduced Jesus to His ministry at His Baptism. With God's Spirit on Him, Jesus openly began His journey to the cross. God the Father here called Jesus His obedient Son and called on everyone to listen to Him.

Jesus is perfect because He is God. He did not need Baptism for forgiveness. He never sinned. Jesus received Baptism "to fulfill all righ-teousness" (Matthew 3:15). He did everything God's Law demands, everything that we are expected to do but cannot because of sin. He took our sin on Himself and was baptized for our forgiveness.

Jesus wanted to be baptized for our sake. He showed that He was ready to take our sins upon Himself. He offered to be the Savior. What Good News for us to share with our family and people everywhere! God's own Son has redeemed us.

Jesus entered His saving ministry for us! He had us in mind when He began to teach and to suffer! That's the Good News of God's perfect plan. Jesus came to serve every sinner.

- **My prayer praising God my Savior for His saving work and my Baptism:**

_____

_____

_____

_____

_____

_____

_____

Sign: _____

Date: _____

Talk about it With My Family

- **Discuss these questions:** What do you remember most about growing up? What do you remember most about growing up in God's family? What does your Baptism mean to you?

- **Make a mural** of John the Baptist baptizing Jesus in the River Jordan. Include the Spirit and the voice of God. Use crayons, pen, pencil, markers, bits of wood, construction paper, and similar materials. When finished, display your work in your home.

With My Mentor

- **Ask your mentor** to discuss contrition and repentance. What does it mean to repent? to be sorry for our sins? Pray together a prayer of confession, and hear God's absolution in Isaiah 43:25. Talk about the meaning of the forgiveness, new life, and eternal salvation you received from God at your Baptism.

- **Read together** Matthew 3:11–17. Share your Baptism anniversary dates, and thank God for His mercy in Jesus.

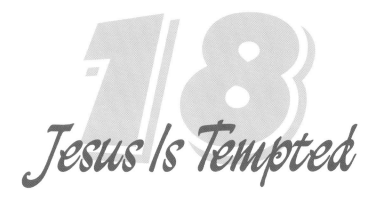

Jesus Is Tempted

The Sixth Petition

And lead us not into temptation.

What does this mean? God tempts no one. We pray in this petition that God would guard and keep us so that the devil, the world, and our sinful nature may not deceive us or mislead us into false belief, despair, and other great shame and vice. Although we are attacked by these things, we pray that we may finally overcome them and win the victory.

Temptations

Temptation can be defined as the attempts of our spiritual enemies to lure us away from God and His ways. The devil, the world, and our sinful nature try to mislead us into false belief, despair, and other sins.

Comparing temptations to birds, Martin Luther once said, "We cannot prevent the birds from flying over our heads, but we can prevent them from building nests in our hair." On the lines below, explain what Luther meant.

_____

_____

_____

_____

_____

_____

Then Jesus was led by the Spirit into the desert to be tempted by the devil. After fasting forty days and forty nights, He was hungry. The tempter came to Him and said, "If You are the Son of God, tell these stones to become bread." Jesus answered, "It is written: 'Man does not live on bread alone, but on every word that comes from the mouth of God.' " Then the devil took Him to the holy city and had Him stand on the highest point of the temple. "If You are the Son of God," he said, "throw Yourself down. For it is written: 'He will command His angels concerning you, and they will lift you up in their hands, so that you will not strike your foot against a stone.' " Jesus answered him, "It is also written: 'Do not put the Lord your God to the test.' " Again, the devil took Him to a very high mountain and showed Him all the kingdoms of the world and their splendor. "All this I will give You," he said, "if You will bow down and worship me." Jesus said to him, "Away from Me, Satan! For it is written: 'Worship the Lord your God, and serve Him only.' " Then the devil left Him, and angels came and attended Him.

Matthew 4:1–11

Into the Desert

1. Why did Satan *tempt Jesus*

a. *with bread?*

_____

_____

_____

b. *with power?*

_____

_____

_____

c. *with riches?*

_____

_____

_____

2. In what ways *does Satan tempt you today?*

_____

_____

_____

_____

God sent His Son to conquer Satan and sin.

Jesus had just been baptized. At the Jordan River, the heavenly Father had revealed His Son as the Savior of the world. Now it was time to begin the battle against Satan. The Holy Spirit led Jesus into the desert to face the devil's temptations.

Satan is still the tempter, a powerful enemy of God's people. He works to separate people from God. Satan wants all people to worship false gods and to reject God's promises. He wants you to depend on yourself and desert God. By tempting Jesus, Satan wanted to keep God's Son from His mission in the world: to save sinners.

The Battle's Won!

In the desert,

Jesus conquered Satan. Armed with God's Word, Jesus resisted Satan's temptations and obeyed His Father. Satan could not deceive Jesus. The Son of God is stronger than all the forces of evil.

Satan plots how he can come between God and His people. He wants to convince us that we can live life doing our own thing. Satan wants us to believe that sin isn't so bad and that we don't need to repent or be forgiven. He tempts us to doubt God and His love for us.

Jesus has conquered Satan for us! Through His victory, we have the strength to resist these temptations. God strengthens and empowers us through His Word to resist the devil's power, just as Jesus did.

Our Weapons

Read the following Bible texts: Genesis 39:9; Job 2:9–10; Proverbs 1:8–16; Luke 4:8; Romans 6:12–18; Romans 13:14. Then choose one or two, and explain why the texts you chose would be of the most help to you in resisting the temptations you face.

_____

_____

_____

_____

Our Support

- Which of the following **do you find especially helpful in your life in resisting the temptations that confront you?**

  ❏ **Reading God's Word**

  ❏ **Remembering Jesus and His love for you**

  ❏ **Having the friendship of those who share your love for Jesus**

  ❏ **Talking with supportive adults who profess their faith in Jesus**

  ❏ **Talking with parents who trust and encourage you**

- What will you say **in your prayers to your heavenly Father today about the help He provides you in your battle against temptation and sin? What will you say to the Savior about His love and forgiveness?**

  _____

  _____

  _____

  Sign: _____

  Date: _____

Talk about it — With My Family

- **Talk about** temptations God's people face today, how we can handle temptations through God's strength, and how we receive God's mercy for our failures. Thank God for His promises.

- **Pray together** asking God to help your family to resist temptation and to remain faithful to our gracious and loving God.

With My Mentor

- **Ask your mentor** about the kinds of temptations he or she faced while growing up. Ask, "In what ways are temptations today similar? different?"

- **Share together**—and memorize—a Bible passage that speaks of God's forgiveness and strength in times of temptation.

Since we have a great high priest who has gone through the heavens, Jesus the Son of God, let us hold firmly to the faith we profess. For we do not have a high priest who is unable to sympathize with our weaknesses, but we have one who has been tempted in every way, just as we are—yet was without sin. Let us then approach the throne of grace with confidence, so that we may receive mercy and find grace to help us in our time of need.

Hebrews 4:14–16

19

Jesus Calls His Disciples

The Second Petition

Thy kingdom come.

What does this mean? The kingdom of God certainly comes by itself without our prayer, but we pray in this petition that it may come to us also.

How does God's kingdom come? God's kingdom comes when our heavenly Father gives us His Holy Spirit, so that by His grace we believe His holy Word and lead godly lives here in time and there in eternity.

The Third Petition

Thy will be done on earth as it is in heaven.

What does this mean? The good and gracious will of God is done even without our prayer, but we pray in this petition that it may be done among us also.

How is God's will done? God's will is done when He breaks and hinders every evil plan and purpose of the devil, the world, and our sinful nature, which do not want us to hallow God's name or let His kingdom come; and when He strengthens and keeps us firm in His Word and faith until we die. This is His good and gracious will.

One day as Jesus was standing by the Lake of Gennesaret, with the people crowding around Him and listening to the word of God, He saw at the water's edge two boats, left there by the fishermen, who were washing their nets. He got into one of the boats, the one belonging to Simon, and asked him to put out a little from shore. Then He sat down and taught the people from the boat. When He had finished speaking, He said to Simon, "Put out into deep water, and let down the nets for a catch."

Simon answered, "Master, we've worked hard all night and haven't caught anything. But because You say so, I will let down the nets."

When they had done so, they caught such a large number of fish that their nets began to break. So they signaled their partners in the other boat to come and help them, and they came and filled both boats so full that they began to sink.

When Simon Peter saw this, he fell at Jesus' knees and said, "Go away from me, Lord; I am a sinful man!" For he and all his companions were astonished at the catch of fish they had taken, and so were James and John, the sons of Zebedee, Simon's partners.

Then Jesus said to Simon, "Don't be afraid; from now on you will catch men." So they pulled their boats up on shore, left everything and followed Him.

Luke 5:1–11

Would You Do It like This?

That's just not the way I'd do it—asking someone who doesn't know anything about baseball to play shortstop. Or asking someone who knows nothing about surgery to do a heart transplant. Then again, I wonder if the first shortstop *did* know anything about baseball. I do believe the first heart transplant surgeon must have studied a long time before doing the first transplant. I wonder why Jesus *did* ask those fishermen to be fishers of men.

I'm an Expert

Everyone has individual strengths and talents. Some excel in sports, while others shine in academics. Still others have a gift for relating to people or for creating works of art, music, or technology. What if you played the trumpet in your school band and the football coach asked you to play quarterback? What if you enjoyed drawing and painting but were asked to represent your school at a math contest? Could you play? Would you go?

- **Think about your strengths and talents. In what areas do you already excel? In what areas would you like to learn to grow?**

- **Strengths and Talents I Have Now**

  _____

  _____

  _____

  _____

- **Strengths and Talents I'd Like to Have**

  _____

  _____

  _____

  _____

Follow Me!

A long time ago, God spoke through Isaiah to announce that the greatest Prophet was still to come.

The Spirit of the Lord is on me,
because He has anointed me
to preach good news to the poor.
He has sent me to proclaim freedom for the prisoners
and recovery of sight for the blind,
to release the oppressed,
to proclaim the year of the Lord's favor.

Luke 4:18–19

Jesus used these words from Isaiah when He spoke in the synagogue at Nazareth. He was the Prophet anointed by God's Spirit to proclaim the Good News! He was sent to set the prisoners free, to give sight to the blind, and to announce God's favor. As He began His ministry, Jesus called people to follow Him. His disciples would travel with Him, learn and listen to His Word, and assist Him in His work of preaching and teaching the Good News.

- **What do you** think it was like to be a fisherman in Jesus' day? Why might Peter have been considered an expert at fishing?

- **Describe Peter's** reaction to the miraculous catch of fish. How did Peter feel in Jesus' presence?

- **Why do you suppose** Jesus called Peter with these words: "From now on you will catch men"?

To Follow Jesus

With My Family

Talk about it

- **Discuss how Jesus** blessed Peter and his companions with an abundant catch of fish. Then talk about ways that Jesus has blessed your family with an "abundant catch of fish."

- **Sometimes adults** don't feel capable of things they are called to do. Ask parents or grandparents what they do when they feel they aren't good enough to do something. What sort of encouragement helps? How do God's forgiveness and strength through Jesus help in difficult situations?

With My Mentor

- **Ask your mentor** what he or she best likes to hear about Jesus. What is the sweetest part of the Gospel to him or her?

- **Ask your mentor** what he or she thinks "Thy kingdom come" means. Ask, "How did God's kingdom come to you? How does it come to you now? What are we asking for when we pray, 'Thy will be done on earth as it is in heaven'?" Share your own ideas about the Second and Third Petitions with your mentor.

Jesus spoke God's Word. As he traveled through Galilee, He called disciples to follow Him. These people left their jobs. They often left their families. Jesus called them to serve in God's kingdom! They were going to share the Gospel—the Good News of forgiveness and life—with a captive, sin-stained people.

We were not there in Galilee to hear Jesus preach and teach or to be called by Jesus personally. Yet Jesus calls us to follow Him too. We are His disciples today who hear His word of salvation and trust Him. Baptized into Jesus' death and resurrection, we live in His kingdom. We serve Him as His followers. Jesus said to Peter, "Do not be afraid; from now on you will be catching men." Jesus calls us and encourages us to share His Good News with others.

- **Who among your family and friends needs to hear about Jesus' love? Write a prayer asking God to use you to share the Gospel with the people you name.**

_____

_____

_____

_____

_____

Sign: _____

Date: _____

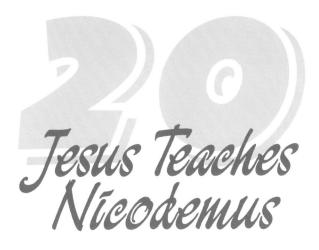

Jesus Teaches Nicodemus

The Nature of Baptism

<u>What is Baptism?</u> Baptism is not just plain water, but it is the water included in God's command and combined with God's word.

<u>Which is that word of God?</u> Christ our Lord says in the last chapter of Matthew: "Therefore go and make disciples of all nations, baptizing them in the name of the Father and of the Son and of the Holy Spirit." [Matt. 28:19]

Great Gifts

"May I go to Kristen's birthday party?" Marshall asked his mother.

"Sure, you may," she said. "Do you want to buy a gift for Kristen by yourself, or do you want me to help you?"

"Do I have to give her a gift?" Marshall asked.

"No, you never *have* to give a gift," said his mother. "If you *had* to give a gift, it wouldn't be a gift."

"Then I don't want to give her anything," Marshall said.

"Why do you think Kristen invited you to her party?" his mother asked.

"Because I'm her friend, I guess," he answered.

"Sometimes people like to invite their friends to parties," said his mother, "and sometimes people like to give their friends birthday gifts."

Now there was a man of the Pharisees named Nicodemus, a member of the Jewish ruling council. He came to Jesus at night and said, "Rabbi, we know You are a teacher who has come from God. For no one could perform the miraculous signs You are doing if God were not with Him."

In reply Jesus declared, "I tell you the truth, no one can see the kingdom of God unless he is born again."

"How can a man be born when he is old?" Nicodemus asked. "Surely he cannot enter a second time into his mother's womb to be born!"

Jesus answered, "I tell you the truth, no one can enter the kingdom of God unless he is born of water and the Spirit. Flesh gives birth to flesh, but the Spirit gives birth to spirit. You should not be surprised at My saying, 'You must be born again.' The wind blows wherever it pleases. You hear its sound, but you cannot tell where it comes from or where it is going. So it is with everyone born of the Spirit."

"How can this be?" Nicodemus asked.

"You are Israel's teacher," said Jesus, "and do you not understand these things? I tell you the truth, we speak of what we know, and we testify to what we have seen, but still you

Continued on page 72

"You mean it's the polite thing to do," Marshall said, knowing his mother was into politeness.

"Yes, it is," said his mother, "but it's more than that. Taking a gift to a party helps you learn how to give. That's an important lesson in life."

"I know how to give, Mom," said Marshall. "You just say, 'Here, I've got something for you.' "

"That's part of it," said his mother, "but you also need to learn how to pick a gift for that special person. You want that person to know that you thought of her. I think it's fun to see someone enjoy a gift that I gave."

"Kristen likes the same kind of music that I do," said Marshall. "I could get her a CD. I know she has a player in her room."

"Would you like to get her a CD?" his mother asked.

"I'll check to see if I have enough money," Marshall said.

- **What gifts have you received that you especially enjoy?**

_____

_____

_____

- **What gifts have you enjoyed giving to others?**

_____

_____

_____

Born Again

Nicodemus was an important man. He served his community as a leader. Although people respected his wisdom and advice, Nicodemus had questions of his own that he needed answered.

Jesus' teaching and preaching led Nicodemus to think about God's kingdom. The reports of miracles caused Nicodemus to seek Jesus out—at night—to talk about God's Word. Nicodemus knew the Holy Scriptures. He believed God's promises to save His people, Israel. The question racing through his mind was simple: Are You, Jesus, the Messiah?

Nicodemus wanted to know and to understand.

Continued from page 71
people do not accept our testimony. I have spoken to you of earthly things and you do not believe; how then will you believe if I speak of heavenly things? No one has ever gone into heaven except the one who came from heaven—the Son of Man. Just as Moses lifted up the snake in the desert, so the Son of Man must be lifted up, that everyone who believes in Him may have eternal life.

"For God so loved the world that He gave His one and only Son, that whoever believes in Him shall not perish but have eternal life."

John 3:1–16

By Water and the Word

Jesus made ordinary water a special blessing when it is used with His Word of grace and promise. He told His disciples to baptize all nations in "the name of the Father and of the Son and of the Holy Spirit." He promised, "He that believes and is baptized shall be saved." St. Paul called the water of this Baptism "the washing of rebirth and renewal by the Holy Spirit, whom He poured out on us generously through Jesus Christ our Savior" (Titus 3:5–6).

Even now God makes us His own children through this Sacrament. God has not removed His power from this sacred act. He who had the power to raise people from the dead also had the power to raise Himself from the dead. Today in Baptism our Lord uses His divine power to give spiritual life to those who are dead in sin. Those who are baptized are born again to a new life. Through His Word and Baptism, He gives us new life, a life in which we think of Him and His love for us each moment.

St. Paul explains: "Don't you know that all of us who were baptized into Christ Jesus were baptized into His death? We were therefore buried with Him through baptism into death in order that, just as Christ was raised from the dead through the glory of the Father, we too may live a new life" (Romans 6:3–4). This is the daily importance of Baptism for the child of God. Our Baptism reminds us every day that God has made us His own dear children. By our daily repentance and sorrow for sin, our sinful self is drowned as if it were held under water. By the power of the Holy Spirit, we arise as a new person with power from God to live according to His will. This is how God makes and keeps us His own.

St. Paul describes Baptism as putting on new clean clothes, the clothes of Christ:

"You are all sons of God through faith in Christ Jesus, for all of you who were baptized into Christ have clothed yourselves with Christ" (Galatians 3:26–27).

- **How does Nicodemus misunderstand Jesus' words about being born again?**

_____

_____

_____

_____

- **What does Jesus mean by "born of water and the Spirit"?**

_____

_____

_____

_____

- **What evidence is there that you have been born again?**

_____

_____

_____

_____

We Are Baptized!

Praise God for making us His children through Baptism! Because of the sinfulness of our first parents, we were born into this world with the desire to rebel against God. At birth original sin separated us from God.

Through Jesus' suffering, death, and resurrection, God rescued us from the power of sin, the devil, and death. Our Lord Jesus conquered all these enemies. He offers and gives us forgiveness of sin and eternal life. In Baptism, He will do what He has promised us—forgive our sins (Acts 2:38–39). Through Baptism, we are brought again into God's family. We can trust Him and His Word of promise always.

Every morning, as we wake up, we remember God is our Father, Jesus is our Savior, and God's Spirit gives power to live as children of God. As we remember our Baptism, every day is a new experience in the grace and love of God.

Jesus wants people of all nations to become God's children through Baptism. As we live the life of a child of God, we join our fellow Christians in telling others of the love of God shown through Jesus' death and resurrection so that they, too, might be brought into His family.

- **Thank You, Lord, for my Baptism. I praise You for**

_____

_____

_____

_____

_____

_____

_____

_____

Sign: _____

Date: _____

Talk about it — With My Family

- **If you were baptized** as a baby or young child, ask a parent to tell you about that special day. Look at pictures, your baby book, or any other memorabilia from that day. Talk about why Baptism is such a special time for your parents and for you. If you know the date of your Baptism, mark it on the calendar so you can remember your re-birthday.

- **Ask your parents** if they remember when they first heard John 3:16. Ask, "What does this passage mean in your life?" Talk about ways you can share the Good News with others in and outside of your family.

With My Mentor

- **Visit a hospital** nursery. Notice how helpless the babies are. Also notice how people smile at them and seem to love them just because they are babies. Talk to your mentor about how God smiles on us—His dear children in Christ—the same way in our Baptism.

- **Ask your mentor** if he or she has ever misunderstood God's Word as Nicodemus did. Share how God teaches and continues to teach us through His Word.

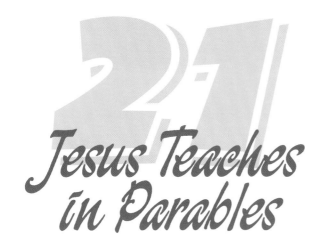

Jesus Teaches in Parables

The Fifth Petition

And forgive us our trespasses as we forgive those who trespass against us.

What does this mean? We pray in this petition that our Father in heaven would not look at our sins, or deny our prayer because of them. We are neither worthy of the things for which we pray, nor have we deserved them, but we ask that He would give them all to us by grace, for we daily sin much and surely deserve nothing but punishment. So we too will sincerely forgive and gladly do good to those who sin against us.

Favorite Stories

"Tell me a story."

A story is simply an account of something happening. A mystery is a story. History is a story too. When you watch a sci-fi film, you are watching a story. When you tell your best friend what happened on your trip, you're telling a story. Everyone loves stories. A good story can teach us things about life, about human nature, and about God.

• **Why do people tell stories? What are your favorite stories? Write the names or titles and a brief summary of the stories.**

_____

_____

_____

Jesus continued: "There was a man who had two sons. The younger one said to his father, 'Father, give me my share of the estate.' So he divided his property between them.

"Not long after that, the younger son got together all he had, set off for a distant country and there squandered his wealth in wild living. After he had spent everything, there was a severe famine in that whole country, and he began to be in need. So he went and hired himself out to a citizen of that country, who sent him to his fields to feed pigs. He longed to fill his stomach with the pods that the pigs were eating, but no one gave him anything.

"When he came to his senses, he said, 'How many of my father's hired men have food to spare, and here I am starving to death! I will set out and go back to my father and say to him: Father, I have sinned against heaven and against you. I am no longer worthy to be called your son; make me like one of your hired men.' So he got up and went to his father.

"But while he was still a long way off, his father saw him and was filled with compassion for him; he ran to his son, threw his arms around him and kissed him.

"The son said to him, 'Father, I have sinned against heaven and against you. I am no longer worthy to be called your son.'

"But the father said to his servants, 'Quick! Bring the best robe and put it on him. Put a ring on his finger and sandals on his feet. Bring the fattened calf and kill it. Let's have a feast and celebrate. For this son of mine was dead and is alive again; he was lost and is found.' So they began to celebrate."

Luke 15:11–24

Parables

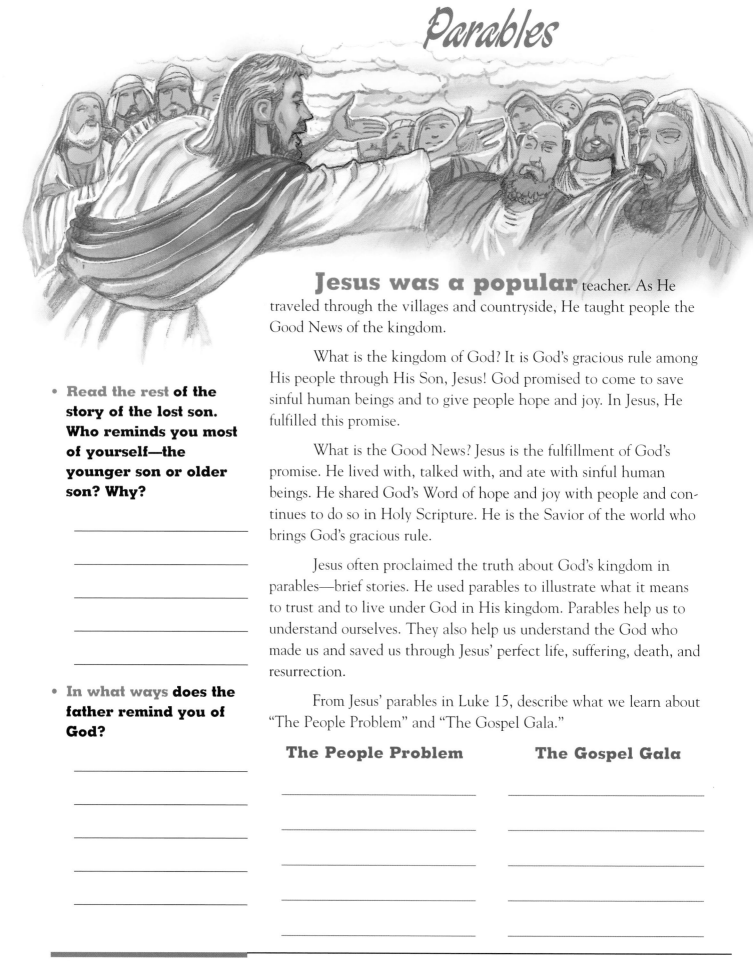

Jesus was a popular teacher. As He traveled through the villages and countryside, He taught people the Good News of the kingdom.

What is the kingdom of God? It is God's gracious rule among His people through His Son, Jesus! God promised to come to save sinful human beings and to give people hope and joy. In Jesus, He fulfilled this promise.

What is the Good News? Jesus is the fulfillment of God's promise. He lived with, talked with, and ate with sinful human beings. He shared God's Word of hope and joy with people and continues to do so in Holy Scripture. He is the Savior of the world who brings God's gracious rule.

Jesus often proclaimed the truth about God's kingdom in parables—brief stories. He used parables to illustrate what it means to trust and to live under God in His kingdom. Parables help us to understand ourselves. They also help us understand the God who made us and saved us through Jesus' perfect life, suffering, death, and resurrection.

From Jesus' parables in Luke 15, describe what we learn about "The People Problem" and "The Gospel Gala."

- **Read the rest of the story of the lost son. Who reminds you most of yourself—the younger son or older son? Why?**

——————————————

——————————————

——————————————

——————————————

——————————————

- **In what ways does the father remind you of God?**

——————————————

——————————————

——————————————

——————————————

——————————————

The People Problem	The Gospel Gala
——————————	——————————
——————————	——————————
——————————	——————————
——————————	——————————
——————————	——————————

Our Father Welcomes

In the media on almost any day you'll find variations on the "lost son" or "lost daughter" theme. Such stories will have headlines similar to these:

- Teen's Parents **Throw Him Out of the House**

- Girl Gets Pregnant **to Punish Parents**

- Teen Boys Arrested **for Physically Abusing Mother and Father**

- "Fights with My Parents **Forced Me to Join a Gang"**

To an outsider, your fights with your parents may seem mild by comparison. To you (and to your parents), family fights cause stress and pain. Left unresolved, anger leads to hate, and hurt feelings lead to resentment, suspicion, and mistrust.

Think of an unresolved argument you had with your parents. Who was responsible? If you answer honestly, you probably have to admit that you shared in the responsibility. You probably also shared in that miserable guilty feeling that hung on in the silence after the storm.

What would it take to resolve the argument and restore the relationship God intended for your family? You may be surprised to discover it will take only five words, but they're the hardest words in the English language to say. Although you would like to hear your parents say these words, the only person you can make say them is you, yourself. Try them on your parents and see what happens.

"I was wrong. I'm sorry."

The lost son in the story Jesus told said those words. As a result, his father killed the fattened calf and hosted a party. His father forgave him. The loving relationship between them was restored.

Jesus told the story to show us that our heavenly Father forgives us and welcomes us home when we confess our sins to Him and tell Him we are sorry. Parents, especially those who share with us our faith in God's love and forgiveness through Jesus, forgive our sins and welcome us home the same way.

With My Family

- **With members** of your family, identify things that would make people want to run away from home. Then make a list of ways family members can help by talking about problems and issues in ways that reflect God's love for us.

- **Prepare a family** feast to celebrate God's love in Jesus. Allow each family member to select a favorite dish. Before your meal, thank God for His blessings on your lives and His forgiveness in Jesus.

With My Mentor

- **Retell the story** of the lost son in today's language; tell the story as if it happened in your neighborhood. Where do the father and his sons live? To where does the son run? How does the father welcome back his son? If possible, write your story and share it with others.

- **Tell about a time** you felt lost. Ask your mentor to do the same. Then share together about the blessings of your Baptism into Christ. Read the baptismal rite in your hymnal. What parts assure you that you are never alone?

The Fifth Petition

We pray in this petition that our Father in heaven would not look at our sins, or deny our prayer because of them. We are neither worthy of the things for which we pray, nor have we deserved them, but we ask that He would give them all to us by grace, for we daily sin much and surely deserve nothing but punishment. So we too will sincerely forgive and gladly do good to those who sin against us.

The Lost Son

- **Write a prayer, thanking God for your forgiveness and life in Christ.**

_____

_____

_____

_____

_____

_____

_____

_____

Sign: _____

Date: _____

Peter Confesses Jesus

The Office of the Keys

What is the Office of the Keys? The Office of the Keys is that special authority which Christ has given to His church on earth to forgive the sins of repentant sinners, but to withhold forgiveness from the unrepentant as long as they do not repent.

Where is this written? This is what St. John the Evangelist writes in chapter twenty: The Lord Jesus breathed on His disciples and said, "Receive the Holy Spirit. If you forgive anyone his sins, they are forgiven; if you do not forgive them, they are not forgiven." [John 20:22–23]

What do you believe according to these words? I believe that when the called ministers of Christ deal with us by His divine command, in particular when they exclude openly unrepentant sinners from the Christian congregation and absolve those who repent of their sins and want to do better, this is just as valid and certain, even in heaven, as if Christ our dear Lord dealt with us Himself.

Different Views

You look different! To different people, you do look different. Your friends look at you in one way; your teacher probably looks at you in a different way. Yet you are still the same person!

Tell how each person might see you in a unique way.

A Team Rival　　　　　　　　**A Teacher**

A Parent　　　　　　　　　　**A Friend**

When Jesus came to the region of Caesarea Philippi, He asked His disciples, "Who do people say the Son of Man is?"

They replied, "Some say John the Baptist; others say Elijah; and still others, Jeremiah or one of the prophets."

"But what about you?" He asked. "Who do you say I am?"

Simon Peter answered, "You are the Christ, the Son of the living God."

Jesus replied, "Blessed are you, Simon son of Jonah, for this was not revealed to you by man, but by My Father in heaven. And I tell you that you are Peter, and on this rock I will build My church, and the gates of Hades will not overcome it. I will give you the keys of the kingdom of heaven; whatever you bind on earth will be bound in heaven, and whatever you loose on earth will be loosed in heaven." Then He warned His disciples not to tell anyone that He was the Christ.

From that time on Jesus began to explain to His disciples that He must go to Jerusalem and suffer many things at the hands of the elders, chief priests and teachers of the law, and that He must be killed and on the third day be raised to life.

Matthew 16:13–21

Right View

1. **Why do people** *have different views about who Jesus is?*

   _____
   _____
   _____
   _____

2. **What message** *about Christ is the foundation of the Church?*

   _____
   _____
   _____
   _____

3. **What are the keys** *of the kingdom (Matthew 16:19)?*

   _____
   _____
   _____
   _____

Jesus taught His disciples. He preached to the crowds in village after village. He healed people with all kinds of sickness and disease. Some people saw Jesus as an excellent teacher; some believed He was a prophet sent by God. The religious leaders of the day, the Pharisees and Sadducees, thought Jesus stirred up trouble in Israel. Different people had different views about Jesus and His mission.

Near the city of Caesarea Philippi, Jesus asked His disciples, "Who do people say I am?" "Some say John the Baptist," the disciples responded. "Some say one of the ancient prophets." Finally Jesus asked the crucial question: *"Who do you say that I am?"*

Peter answered, "You are the Christ, the Son of the living God." It was an answer inspired by God. Just as the heavenly Father had revealed Jesus as His beloved Son at His Baptism, so the heavenly Father gave Peter a wonderful answer about who Jesus is (Matthew 16:17). He is the Christ, the Son of the living God. He is the promised Messiah, the Savior, the Church's one foundation.

The Holy Christian Church

"I believe in the holy Christian church, the communion of saints." Christians confess this belief in the words of the Apostles' Creed. The Church is Christian because our Lord founded the Church. He is the Christ, the Messiah, the Anointed One of God who completed the work of salvation. Whoever believes and confesses "Jesus Christ is my Lord" is a member of the communion of saints, the Christian Church.

Jesus chose twelve men to teach and proclaim the Gospel of salvation. Not only were these apostles to announce the forgiveness of sin, which unlocks the door of heaven, but they were also to warn of eternal death to impenitent sinners. When sinners want to stay in their sin and refuse to believe the Gospel, the door to heaven is locked to them.

The Christian Church is made up of all people who believe and confess "Jesus Christ is my Lord." Jesus gives the believers in the Church the power to proclaim and apply the Gospel of forgiveness, which unlocks the door to heaven, and to warn against impenitence, which locks heaven's door.

The Church—My Family

With My Family

- **If guests came** to your home, would they see that Jesus is the most important person in your family? Plan together to decorate your house in ways that show Jesus is your Lord and Savior. When guests visit, use the decorations to begin conversations about your Savior.

- **As a family,** plant a fruit tree in your yard. Talk about what kind you will plant, where you'll plant it, and how you'll take care of it. When you have made your plans, plant it together. As you are planting, talk about the fruit that it will one day bear. Thank God for the fruit of the Holy Spirit—love, joy, peace, patience, kindness, faithfulness, gentleness, and self-control. Talk about how God gives these gifts to members of His Church through the means of grace.

With My Mentor

- **Read together** the Third Article and its explanation. Discuss ways that you can encourage each other to trust in Jesus as your Savior.

- **Ask your mentor** to share a story about a time when telling someone they were forgiven for Jesus' sake brought blessing to that person. Share your own story about God's forgiveness and mercy in your life.

We believe that Jesus Christ is Lord. We make this confession because God's Holy Spirit has called us by the Gospel. He has given us the only faith that saves. We can be sure that we are His children because He made us members of the Church by Baptism.

We believe in the holy Christian Church, the communion of saints. We belong to God's family together with all people who have been called by the Gospel. Jesus promises us that His Church will last forever.

Jesus asked Peter and the disciples, "Who do you say I am?"

Who do I say You are, Jesus?
You are

_____

_____

_____

_____

_____

_____

_____

_____

Sign: _____

Date: _____

Jesus Raises Lazarus

The Second Article

I believe . . . in Jesus Christ, His only Son, our Lord, who was conceived by the Holy Spirit, born of the Virgin Mary, suffered under Pontius Pilate, was crucified, died and was buried. He descended into hell. The third day He rose again from the dead. He ascended into heaven and sits at the right hand of God, the Father Almighty. From thence He will come to judge the living and the dead.

What does this mean? I believe that Jesus Christ, true God, begotten of the Father from eternity, and also true man, born of the Virgin Mary, is my Lord, who has redeemed me, a lost and condemned person, purchased and won me from all sins, from death, and from the power of the devil; not with gold or silver, but with His holy, precious blood and with His innocent suffering and death, that I may be His own and live under Him in His kingdom and serve Him in everlasting righteousness, innocence, and blessedness, just as He is risen from the dead, lives and reigns to all eternity. This is most certainly true.

"Lord," Martha said to Jesus, "if You had been here, my brother would not have died. But I know that even now God will give You whatever You ask." Jesus said to her, "Your brother will rise again." Martha answered, "I know he will rise again in the resurrection at the last day." Jesus said to her, "I am the resurrection and the life. He who believes in Me will live, even though he dies; and whoever lives and believes in Me will never die. Do you believe this?"

"Yes, Lord," she told Him, "I believe that You are the Christ, the Son of God, who was to come into the world." . . .

So they took away the stone. Then Jesus looked up and said, "Father, I thank You that You have heard Me. I knew that You always hear Me, but I said this for the benefit of the people standing here, that they may believe that You sent Me."

When He had said this, Jesus called in a loud voice, "Lazarus, come out!" The dead man came out, his hands and feet wrapped with strips of linen, and a cloth around his face.

Jesus said to them, "Take off the grave clothes and let him go."

John 11:21–27, 41–44

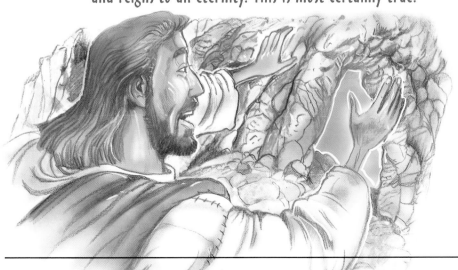

A Friend in Need

- **Check boxes in front of any of the following statements that, in your opinion, describe someone who is a true friend.**

A true friend . . .

- ☐ spends time **with you.**
- ☐ feels with you **and for you.**
- ☐ likes many **of the same things you do.**
- ☐ shares with **you.**
- ☐ does things **with you.**
- ☐ does things **for you.**
- ☐ lets you know **you are a valued person.**
- ☐ willingly takes **the punishment and humiliation you deserve.**
- ☐ would not let **even death stand in the way of your friendship.**

1. **In what ways** *are you like Lazarus?*

   _____
   _____
   _____
   _____

2. **In what ways** *are you like Mary, Martha, and other people in this story?*

   _____
   _____
   _____
   _____

3. **What has Jesus** *done to give you life?*

   _____
   _____
   _____
   _____

Lord of Life

Jesus is Lord of life. He begins life. He preserves life. During His ministry on earth, He even restored life to people who had died.

Jairus's daughter died. The girl was only twelve years old, and her father was an important leader in his community. When death came to Jairus's daughter, Jesus, the Lord of life, raised the girl to life!

The son of a widow from Nain also died. He was an only son; the widow would now live alone. Jesus and His disciples met the funeral procession on the way out of the city.

When Jesus saw what had happened, the compassionate Savior spoke His powerful words, "Young man, I say to you, get up!" (Luke 7:14). As the Lord of life, Jesus restored life to a mother and her son.

The story of the raising of Lazarus also shows Jesus' remarkable power over sin, death, and the power of the devil. The Savior of the world is the Lord of the universe who brings life.

Full Life

God made people to live. He never intended that they should die. When Adam and Eve sinned, death became part of our existence. Now because all people sin, all people must die.

Since God originally created people to live, to die is unnatural. Death is the penalty for sin, the last enemy for people to overcome.

Jesus raised people from the dead, showing that He is the Lord of life. He overcame death for us when He died on the cross and arose again from the dead. When God calls people to have faith in Jesus, He gives them spiritual life. They live close to God forever. This is the full life that Jesus gives to those who trust in Him.

"The wages of sin is death" (Romans 6:23). Eternal death is the punishment we deserve because we are sinners. In love, however, God gives to us the free gift of eternal life. God grants this life through faith in Jesus. He assures us that He has forgiven our sin through His death on the cross. He promises that we will rise from the dead because of His resurrection. He is our resurrection and life.

By the power of the Holy Spirit, we trust Jesus in life and in death. He is our strength against temptations to sin. He helps us overcome our fear of dying. He promises to take us into His presence to be with God forever.

- **Life is precious.** **Every day is a gift of our Savior God. Write a prayer of thanksgiving for your full life in Christ.**

_____

_____

_____

_____

_____

_____

_____

Sign: _____

Date: _____

With My Family

- **Talk together** about the death of someone close to your family. How did your family respond to this death? What Christian comfort did you share with others? Is there anything you could have done differently? What? Why?

- **Discuss with your** family the hymns and Scripture readings you would like to have included in your funeral service.

With My Mentor

- **Take a trip to** a cemetery. Discuss your thoughts and feelings as you view the information on the headstones. What is your predominant feeling? Do you or your mentor know why? Discuss what words of Christian joy you might want on your gravestone.

- **When are the times** when you feel most "alive"? Can you identify the common factors that contribute to this heightened awareness of life and what it has to offer? How does knowing your sins are forgiven through Jesus increase your joy?

Jesus Enters Jerusalem

As they approached Jerusalem and came to Bethphage and Bethany at the Mount of Olives, Jesus sent two of His disciples, saying to them, "Go to the village ahead of you, and just as you enter it, you will find a colt tied there, which no one has ever ridden. Untie it and bring it here. If anyone asks you, 'Why are you doing this?' tell him, 'The Lord needs it and will send it back here shortly.' "

They went and found a colt outside in the street, tied at a doorway. As they untied it, some people standing there asked, "What are you doing, untying that colt?" They answered as Jesus had told them to, and the people let them go. When they brought the colt to Jesus and threw their cloaks over it, He sat on it. Many people spread their cloaks on the road, while others spread branches they had cut in the fields. Those who went ahead and those who followed shouted,

"Hosanna!"

"Blessed is He who comes in the name of the Lord!"

"Blessed is the coming kingdom of our father David!"

"Hosanna in the highest!"

Mark 11:1–10

The Conclusion to the Lord's Prayer

For Thine is the kingdom and the power and the glory forever and ever. Amen.

What does this mean? This means that I should be certain that these petitions are pleasing to our Father in heaven, and are heard by Him; for He Himself has commanded us to pray in this way and has promised to hear us. Amen, amen means "yes, yes, it shall be so."

The Ride

The line snaked through the barriers and around the corner. _Thirty minutes from this point._ Mike and Julie would have to wait. Soon, however, it would be their turn —a quadruple looping, feet dangling, upside down, seems-like-90-miles-an-hour rush of screams and laughter. The best roller-coaster ride ever. They waited, at times impatiently, always with great anticipation. Finally, they were next. They sat down quickly before the safety harnesses were lowered in place. "No going back!" shouted Julie.

• **Describe the most exciting ride you have experienced.**

_____

_____

_____

_____

The Triumphal Entry

Imagine what Jesus' ride was like. Imagine you are on the outskirts of Jerusalem, watching His entry into the city.

1. What might Jesus have been thinking as He saw people along the way?

_____
_____
_____
_____

2. Why do you think the people gathered that day to see Him?

_____
_____
_____
_____

3. Explain the meaning of the words the people shouted.

_____
_____
_____
_____

One Sunday, the people of Jerusalem saw a thrilling parade.

The day before, Jesus had stayed in the home of Mary, Martha, and Lazarus in Bethany. When it was time to go to Jerusalem with His disciples, Jesus did not walk into the city. He rode a donkey.

As He rode into Jerusalem, Jesus was greeted by a cheering crowd. For hundreds of years, God's people had waited for this special ride. Long ago the prophet Zechariah promised, "Rejoice greatly, O Daughter of Zion! Shout, Daughter of Jerusalem! See, your king comes to you, righ- teous and having salvation, gentle and riding on a donkey, on a colt, the foal of a donkey" (Zechariah 9:9).

Redeemer King

Jesus' ride into Jerusalem is the

story of the first Palm Sunday. His entrance into the city—humbly on a donkey—was filled with joy and expectation. The crowds of people confessed that He was the Son of David. Jesus was their King! When they shouted, "Hosanna!" they were saying, "Lord, save us!"

In reality, Jesus was not a powerful ruler in this world. He was the suffering Savior, sent by God to die on a cross.

Beginning with His Baptism and continuing through His ride into Jerusalem, Jesus fulfilled the will of His Father. He traveled the path that showed God's ultimate love for His people. It is a path that leads to forgiveness, life, and salvation.

Today, by faith, we see Jesus enter Jerusalem as our Redeemer King. The Son of God listened to the shouts of praise, "Hosanna! Blessed is He who comes in the name of the Lord!" Just days later, He also listened to crowds cry out, "Crucify Him!" He died willingly, freely, for us. His resurrection was His cry of "Yes, yes, it shall be so."

Jesus is our King. He conquered all our enemies. He has promised to keep us in His kingdom here on earth and to take us to His heavenly kingdom forever. Jesus is our Lord and Savior, the King and Ruler of the universe. We can ask God anything in His name.

- **Write a brief prayer, thanking Jesus for His love and for making you a member of His kingdom and for the privilege of coming to God in prayer in His name, confident that He hears and answers our prayers.**

_____

_____

_____

_____

_____

_____

Sign: _____

Date: _____

Talk about it — With My Family

- **What kinds of activities** do you do together as a family that show you are members of the kingdom of God through faith in Christ Jesus? What kinds of activities could be done together that would provide this opportunity?

- **What things evidence** the almighty power and majesty of God? Talk about how these things give you hope and confidence as you think about your identity as a Christian.

With My Mentor

- **Share together** some of the faith events in your life since your Baptism. Then pray the Lord's Prayer together.

- **Talk together** about the prayers you have offered and the answers you have received from God, who possesses all control and power and glory.

Jesus the Servant

Confession and Absolution

What is Confession? Confession has two parts. First, that we confess our sins, and second, that we receive absolution, that is, forgiveness, from the pastor as from God Himself, not doubting, but firmly believing that by it our sins are forgiven before God in heaven.

What sins should we confess? Before God we should plead guilty of all sins, even those we are not aware of, as we do in the Lord's Prayer; but before the pastor we should confess only those sins which we know and feel in our hearts.

What's the Next Step?

Cindy and Brad both felt disappointed in themselves. They knew their mother was disappointed in them too. She had come home late Saturday to a house full of unwashed clothes, messy bedrooms, and dirty dishes. And all this even though they had promised to do their household chores if they were allowed to go out with their friends that Saturday morning.

What action might Cindy and Brad take first, given how they feel about the situation they have created?

What action might they take as an appropriate step after that?

The evening meal was being served, and the devil had already prompted Judas Iscariot, son of Simon, to betray Jesus. Jesus knew that the Father had put all things under His power, and that He had come from God and was returning to God; so He got up from the meal, took off His outer clothing, and wrapped a towel around His waist. After that, He poured water into a basin and began to wash His disciples' feet, drying them with the towel that was wrapped around Him. He came to Simon Peter, who said to Him, "Lord, are You going to wash my feet?"

Jesus replied, "You do not realize now what I am doing, but later you will understand."

"No," said Peter, "You shall never wash my feet."

Jesus answered, "Unless I wash you, you have no part with Me."

"Then, Lord," Simon Peter replied, "not just my feet but my hands and my head as well!"

Jesus answered, "A person who has had a bath needs only to wash his feet; his whole body is clean. And you are clean, though not every one of you." For He knew who was going to betray Him, and that was why He said not every one was clean.

When He had finished washing their feet, He put on His clothes and returned to His place. "Do you understand what I have done for you?" He asked them. "You call Me 'Teacher' and 'Lord,' and rightly so, for that is what I am. Now that I, your Lord and Teacher, have washed your feet, you also should wash one another's feet. I have set you an example that you should do as I have done for you."

John 13:2–15

A Humble Servant

Jesus is King of all, but He is also a Servant. On Palm Sunday, Jesus grandly entered Jerusalem. On Thursday, Jesus was a Servant.

He and the twelve apostles ate supper together in a quiet room in the home of a friend of Jesus. As they were eating this Passover meal together, Jesus rose, took off His robe, and laid it aside. He tied a towel around His waist and poured water into a bowl. As the startled disciples watched, Jesus began to wash their feet and wipe them with a towel.

Jesus must have surprised His apostles when He began to wash their feet. He was their Master, but He did something only a servant should do. Jesus was a King, but in humility He came to serve, not to be served.

He did the servant's job for His disciples because He loved them dearly. His action made Peter confess that he needed to have his whole person washed. Before the next day ended, the disciples would see Jesus' greatest act of servant love. He would die on the cross to take away their sins and ours. Now we come to Him to confess our sins and receive the assurance of forgiveness. God's Word records, "If we confess our sins, He is faithful and just and will forgive us our sins and purify us from all unrighteousness" (1 John 1:9).

1. **Describe Jesus'** *love shown in the foot washing.*

_____

_____

_____

2. **Why did Peter ask** *to have his whole person washed? How are these thoughts and feelings related to confession?*

_____

_____

_____

3. **What would you** *think if Jesus washed your feet today?*

_____

_____

_____

Called to Serve

God has called us into His kingdom to serve others. Our King, Jesus Christ, Teacher and Lord, was also our Servant. His sacrificial service to us calls us to serve others. His example of washing the disciples' feet reminds us of the many ways we can serve other people. One way is to remind those troubled over their sins that Jesus has paid the penalty for all sins. We are forgiven!

When we were baptized, Jesus brought us into His family. Jesus' love and power moves us to serve others in His name.

• **When I think about serving Christ, I want to . . .**

_____

_____

_____

_____

_____

_____

Sign: _____

Date: _____

Talk about it — With My Family

• **Discuss a time** when you should have confessed a sin and didn't. Ask people in your family if they have ever done the same thing. Ask how the story of Jesus washing His disciples' feet encourages people to confess when they do wrong things. Pray together for strength to confess sins to one another.

• **Privately make a list** of things you can do to serve the members of your family and to show your love for Jesus. Then, without telling anyone, do these things and watch for their response.

With My Mentor

• **Ask and discuss,** "Has confessing sins been a big part of your life? What is the benefit of confessing to someone you have wronged? What words do you use to tell someone he is forgiven? What words does the Church use to assure you that your sins are forgiven in Christ?"

• **With your mentor,** plan a servant project the two of you can do together.

When the hour came, Jesus and His apostles reclined at the table. And He said to them, "I have eagerly desired to eat this Passover with you before I suffer. For I tell you, I will not eat it again until it finds fulfillment in the kingdom of God." . . .

And He took bread, gave thanks and broke it, and gave it to them, saying, "This is My body given for you; do this in remembrance of Me."

In the same way, after the supper He took the cup, saying, "This cup is the new covenant in My blood, which is poured out for you. But the hand of him who is going to betray Me is with Mine on the table. The Son of Man will go as it has been decreed, but woe to that man who betrays Him." They began to question among themselves which of them it might be who would do this.

Also a dispute arose among them as to which of them was considered to be greatest. Jesus said to them, "The kings of the Gentiles lord it over them; and those who exercise authority over them call themselves Benefactors. But you are not to be like that. Instead, the greatest among you should be like the youngest, and the one who rules like the one who serves. For who is greater, the one who is at the table or the one who serves? Is it not the one who is at the table? But I am among you as one who serves."

Luke 22:14–16, 19–27

26

Jesus Gives the Lord's Supper

The Nature and Benefit of the Sacrament of the Altar

What is the Sacrament of the Altar? It is the true body and blood of our Lord Jesus Christ under the bread and wine, instituted by Christ Himself for us Christians to eat and to drink.

Where is this written? The holy Evangelists Matthew, Mark, Luke, and St. Paul write: Our Lord Jesus Christ, on the night when He was betrayed, took bread, and when He had given thanks, He broke it and gave it to the disciples and said: "Take, eat; this is My body, which is given for you. This do in remembrance of Me." In the same way also He took the cup after supper, and when He had given thanks, He gave it to them, saying, "Drink of it, all of you; this cup is the new testament in My blood, which is shed for you for the forgiveness of sins. This do, as often as you drink it, in remembrance of Me."

What is the benefit of this eating and drinking? These words, "Given and shed for you for the forgiveness of sins," show us that in the Sacrament forgiveness of sins, life, and salvation are given us through these words. For where there is forgiveness of sins, there is also life and salvation.

A Special Event

R. D. Castoni Birthday Observed

A large gathering of family and friends helped business and community leader R. D. Castoni observe his ninety-fifth birthday at the Middale Community Center on Saturday. Following a number of speeches by business associates, friends, and family members, Mr. Castoni addressed the group. Characteristically, he spoke of his family and friends and of his love and concern for everyone. The group then enjoyed a delicious buffet meal featuring several of Mr. Castoni's favorite dishes. An Italian immigrant with humble beginnings, R. D. Castoni founded Castoni, Inc., in 1956.

Mr. Castoni's Birthday Observation

Person honored

_____

Food served

_____

Those present

_____

Significance of event

_____

The Lord's Supper

Person honored

_____

Food served

_____

Those present

_____

Significance of event

_____

The Lord's Supper

Jesus gave His people a precious gift before He died. This gift is His Holy Supper.

It happened the night Jesus shared the Passover meal with His disciples. For many hundreds of years, God's people remembered the time when the blood of the Passover lamb had saved lives. God saved Israel by directing the angel of death to "pass over" the houses of those who had the blood of a lamb painted on their door posts. By this action, God freed them from the angel of death and from slavery in Egypt. Each year the Israelites ate the Passover meal to celebrate that great event.

On the Thursday night before His crucifixion, Jesus and His disciples ate the Passover meal. While they were eating, Jesus took some of the bread, prayed a prayer of thanks, and broke the bread in pieces.

"Take, eat," He said as He gave it to the disciples. "This is My body. It is given for you."

Then He took a cup of wine. Again He prayed a thanksgiving prayer and gave it to the disciples.

"Drink of it, all of you. This is My blood of the new covenant. It is poured out for the forgiveness of your sins. Each time you celebrate this Holy Supper, you shall remember Me and My work of redemption."

- **If I were Jesus' disciple I would think . . .**

  _____

  _____

  _____

- **If I were Jesus' disciple I would say . . .**

  _____

  _____

  _____

- **If I had been present at the Lord's Supper I would have thought and said . . .**

  _____

  _____

  _____

Real Presence

To this very day, Christians remember the death of the Lord Jesus Christ by eating this sacred meal. When we come to the altar to partake of Holy Communion, Jesus is present to serve us Himself. In this wonderful way, He gives us His body and blood for the forgiveness of our sins.

Jesus replaced the Passover meal of the old covenant with His Holy Supper in the new covenant. God's people of the Old Testament found strength in remembering the act of God through the blood of the Passover lamb. God's people of the New Testament remember the sacrifice of the Lamb of God, Jesus Christ.

We cannot explain how we receive Jesus' body and blood in this Holy Supper. We simply believe Jesus when He promises to be present in the bread and wine for the forgiveness of all our sins. He makes our faith strong when we receive His body and blood in the Sacrament.

- **You have an exchange** student from Japan living with you. Although she is a Buddhist, she goes to church with you. After having gone for several Sundays, she says, "I want to go to the Holy Meal too." What would you say? What would you do? What might she say?

- **You have just had** an argument with your mother. Now it's over, and you've said that you are sorry. She says, "There's Communion today. Are you going?" What would you say? What would you do?

- **You and your friend** are both going to confirmation class. You have just finished studying the Lord's Supper. You will be ready to go to Communion soon. How might you feel? How might your friend feel? What might you say to each other?

- **What do you expect** to receive from God when you receive Holy Communion? For which words will you especially listen?

For You!

With My Family

- **The Passover meal** that Jesus celebrated is a meal of remembrance. Talk about special meals that your family remembers. What made them special? Were you remembering an event in your family? Thank God for the blessing of memories.

- **As a family,** start a new tradition. On Communion Sundays, before you leave the house, take turns forgiving one another's sins. Be sure to tell each other, "I forgive you because Jesus forgives me."

With My Mentor

- **Ask your mentor** to tell why Holy Communion is important to him or her. Talk about any ways you can personally prepare for receiving the Sacrament. Perhaps you and your mentor can have a devotion with your pastor before you receive the Lord's Supper.

- **Ask your mentor** about times that Holy Communion has been especially important. Ask him or her to share with you times that they particularly felt that God's strength through the power of the Holy Spirit in the Sacrament helped them through a difficult time in their life.

Every time your congregation celebrates Holy Communion, God makes it a happy event. He brings Jesus' saving death on the cross into the life of each believer. Jesus says, "This is for you. I shed My blood for you. I forgive all your sins." Jesus gives His body and blood in and with the bread and wine. He Himself is present to reveal the love God has for us.

We are thankful to God for bringing His people together to share His love in this Supper.

- **The Lord's Supper is . . .**

  _____

  _____

- **The Lord's Supper gives . . .**

  _____

  _____

- **I thank You, Lord Jesus, for Your supper because . . .**

  _____

  _____

  Sign: _____

  Date: _____

27

Jesus Is Condemned and Crucified

The Power of the Sacrament of the Altar

How can bodily eating and drinking do such great things? Certainly not just eating and drinking do these things, but the words written here: "Given and shed for you for the forgiveness of sins." These words, along with the bodily eating and drinking, are the main thing in the Sacrament. Whoever believes these words has exactly what they say: "forgiveness of sins."

Worthily Receiving the Sacrament

Who receives this sacrament worthily? Fasting and bodily preparation are certainly fine outward training. But that person is truly worthy and well prepared who has faith in these words: "Given and shed for you for the forgiveness of sins." But anyone who does not believe these words or doubts them is unworthy and unprepared, for the words "for you" require all hearts to believe.

It was the third hour when they crucified Him. The written notice of the charge against Him read: THE KING OF THE JEWS. They crucified two robbers with Him, one on His right and one on His left. Those who passed by hurled insults at Him, shaking their heads and saying, "So! You who are going to destroy the temple and build it in three days, come down from the cross and save Yourself!"

In the same way the chief priests and the teachers of the law mocked Him among themselves. "He saved others," they said, "but He can't save Himself! Let this Christ, this King of Israel, come down now from the cross, that we may see and believe." Those crucified with Him also heaped insults on Him.

At the sixth hour darkness came over the whole land until the ninth hour. And at the ninth hour Jesus cried out in a loud voice, "Eloi, Eloi, lama sabachthani?"—which means, "My God, My God, why have You forsaken Me?"

When some of those standing near heard this, they said, "Listen, He's calling Elijah." One man ran, filled a sponge with wine vinegar, put it on a stick, and offered it to Jesus to drink. "Now leave Him alone. Let's see if Elijah comes to take Him down," he said. With a loud cry, Jesus breathed His last.

The curtain of the temple was torn in two from top to bottom. And when the centurion, who stood there in front of Jesus, heard His cry and saw how He died, he said, "Surely this man was the Son of God!"

Mark 15:25–39

Alone

Complete the T-chart below to describe your thoughts on being alone.

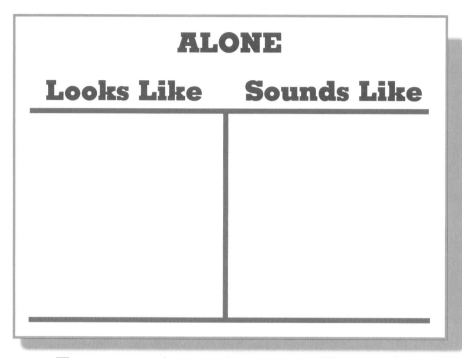

There are times when we value our privacy. There are other times when we despair of being alone. At one critical moment in history, Jesus was completely alone, abandoned by even His Father in heaven.

Condemned!

"He is worthy of death!"

1. Why did Jesus *remain silent when He was falsely accused?*

_____

_____

_____

_____

2. When did Jesus *answer His enemies?*

_____

_____

_____

_____

These words were spoken by the council, the religious leaders of Jesus' day. False witnesses brought charges against Jesus. "He speaks against the temple. He teaches contrary to our laws." Even when the witnesses' statements did not agree, Jesus remained silent.

Finally the high priest demanded, "Are You the Christ, the Son of the Blessed One?"

Jesus' answer was clear: "I am, and you will see the Son of Man seated at the right hand of the Mighty One, and coming with the clouds of heaven."

The high priest then asked the council, "What is your decision?"

They all condemned Him to death.

Crucified!

Pilate's soldiers led Jesus away to crucify Him. They made Him carry His own cross. He was tired and weak because He had suffered so much. Along the way, the cross became too heavy for Him. He stumbled and fell.

A soldier called to a man in the crowd, "Come and carry this cross!" The man was Simon from Cyrene. He carried the cross for Jesus the rest of the way.

Leaving Jerusalem, the crowd followed Jesus to a hill called Golgotha, which means "place of a skull." Here the soldiers nailed Him to the cross and stood it upright in the ground. Two other men were crucified there also. They were robbers. Jesus spoke seven times from the cross. On the lines to the right describe what each statement reveals about Jesus' love for God and for others.

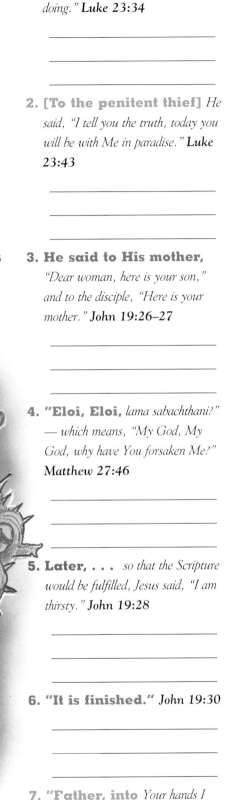

1. **"Father, forgive them,** *for they do not know what they are doing." Luke 23:34*

   _____

   _____

   _____

2. **[To the penitent thief]** *He said, "I tell you the truth, today you will be with Me in paradise." Luke 23:43*

   _____

   _____

   _____

3. **He said to His mother,** *"Dear woman, here is your son," and to the disciple, "Here is your mother." John 19:26–27*

   _____

   _____

   _____

4. **"Eloi, Eloi,** *lama sabachthani?" — which means, "My God, My God, why have You forsaken Me?" Matthew 27:46*

   _____

   _____

   _____

5. **Later, . . .** *so that the Scripture would be fulfilled, Jesus said, "I am thirsty." John 19:28*

   _____

   _____

   _____

6. **"It is finished."** John 19:30

   _____

   _____

   _____

7. **"Father, into** *Your hands I commit My spirit!" Luke 23:46*

   _____

   _____

   _____

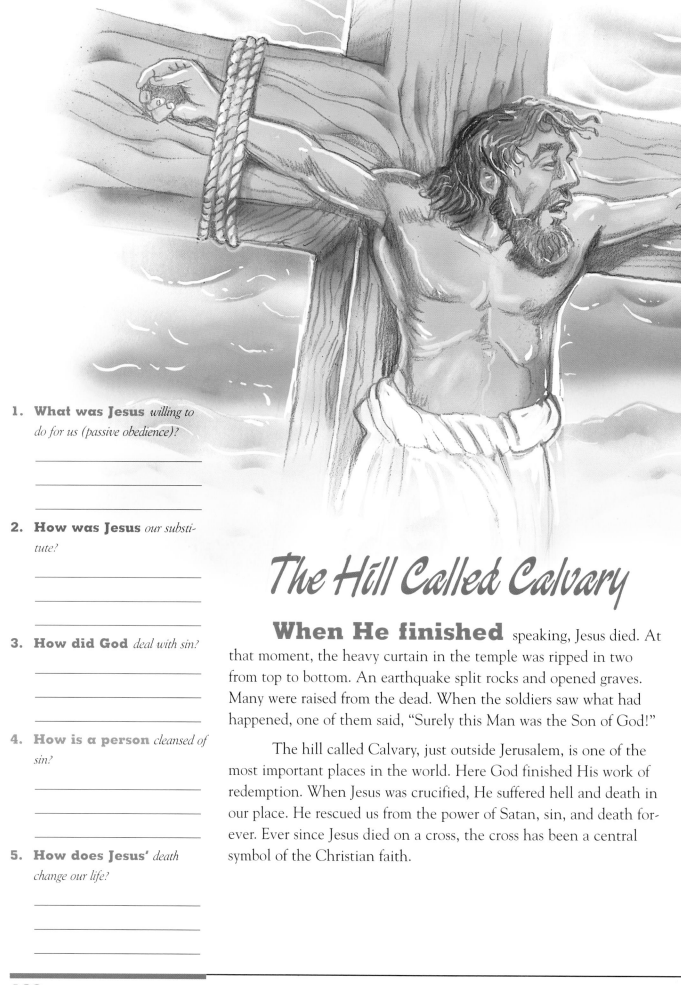

1. **What was Jesus** *willing to do for us (passive obedience)?*

_____
_____
_____

2. **How was Jesus** *our substitute?*

_____
_____
_____

3. **How did God** *deal with sin?*

_____
_____
_____

4. **How is a person** *cleansed of sin?*

_____
_____
_____

5. **How does Jesus'** *death change our life?*

_____
_____
_____

The Hill Called Calvary

When He finished speaking, Jesus died. At that moment, the heavy curtain in the temple was ripped in two from top to bottom. An earthquake split rocks and opened graves. Many were raised from the dead. When the soldiers saw what had happened, one of them said, "Surely this Man was the Son of God!"

The hill called Calvary, just outside Jerusalem, is one of the most important places in the world. Here God finished His work of redemption. When Jesus was crucified, He suffered hell and death in our place. He rescued us from the power of Satan, sin, and death forever. Ever since Jesus died on a cross, the cross has been a central symbol of the Christian faith.

Our Conqueror

Praise God! He sent His Son to conquer sin, death, and the devil for us. When Jesus suffered and died on the cross, He completed His work of rescuing us from the power of Satan, sin, and death. When we receive Jesus' very body and blood together with the bread and wine at the Lord's Supper, we receive also the assurance of our forgiveness and salvation and the strength to live our lives for Jesus.

God protects us from Satan's temptations. He gives us the strength to live as His children. In Jesus' crucifixion, death, and resurrection, we, too, conquer sin and death, and we look forward to eternal life in heaven.

We receive Jesus' body and blood in the Lord's Supper worthily when we believe the words "for you."

- **Write a prayer thanking Jesus for His victory over sin for you.**

_____

_____

_____

_____

Sign: _____

Date: _____

Talk about it — With My Family

- **Make a cross** for your table. Use it as a centerpiece to remind you of Jesus' love for you and of the restored relationship you now enjoy with your heavenly Father as His redeemed and restored child.

- **Read or sing** together a Holy Week hymn. Talk about the words of each stanza with your family.

With My Mentor

- **Talk with your mentor** about the peace that comes from knowing Jesus as your Savior. Ask your mentor to share with you about the peace he or she receives in Holy Communion.

- **Ask your mentor** to tell you how he or she prepares to receive the Lord's Supper. Then ask about how receiving the Lord's Supper helps Christians deal with feelings of loneliness.

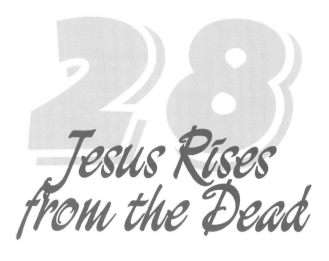

Jesus Rises from the Dead

After the Sabbath, at dawn on the first day of the week, Mary Magdalene and the other Mary went to look at the tomb. There was a violent earthquake, for an angel of the Lord came down from heaven and, going to the tomb, rolled back the stone and sat on it. His appearance was like lightning, and his clothes were white as snow. The guards were so afraid of him that they shook and became like dead men.

The angel said to the women, "Do not be afraid, for I know that you are looking for Jesus, who was crucified. He is not here; He has risen, just as He said. Come and see the place where He lay. Then go quickly and tell His disciples: 'He has risen from the dead and is going ahead of you into Galilee. There you will see Him.' Now I have told you."

So the women hurried away from the tomb, afraid yet filled with joy, and ran to tell His disciples. Suddenly Jesus met them. "Greetings," He said. They came to Him, clasped His feet and worshiped Him. Then Jesus said to them, "Do not be afraid. Go and tell My brothers to go to Galilee; there they will see Me."

Matthew 28:1–10

What Baptism Indicates

What does such baptizing with water indicate? It indicates that the Old Adam in us should by daily contrition and repentance be drowned and die with all sins and evil desires, and that a new man should daily emerge and arise to live before God in righteousness and purity forever.

Law and Gospel

Where alone does God offer the forgiveness of sins? God offers the forgiveness of sins only in the Gospel, the good news that we are freed from the guilt, the punishment, and the power of sin, and are saved eternally because of Christ's keeping the Law and His suffering and death for us.

What is the difference between the Law and the Gospel? The Law teaches what we are to do and not to do; the Gospel teaches what God has done, and still does, for our salvation. The Law shows us our sin and the wrath of God; the Gospel shows us our Savior and the grace of God. The Law must be proclaimed to all people, but especially to impenitent sinners; the Gospel must be proclaimed to sinners who are troubled in their minds because of their sins.

We Thought You Were Dead!
Soldiers in Elizabethtown,

Kentucky, were watching a live television news report. The report showed American prisoners returning to the United States from Operation Desert Storm in Iraq. One of their friends, a pilot, had been shot down, and they thought he had died in the crash. As they watched the TV report, they saw him getting off a plane. There were shouts of surprise, excitement, and celebration. They thought he was dead, but they could see that he really was alive!

He Is Alive!

Jesus' friends watched Him die on the cross. Then a man by the name of Joseph, from the city of Arimathea, asked Pilate for permission to care for the body of Jesus. Pilate told him he could take Jesus' body from the cross and bury it. That same day, Joseph wrapped Jesus' body in a linen sheet. He laid Jesus' body in his own tomb, which was cut out of rock. No one else had ever been buried there.

Some women had followed Jesus from Galilee to Jerusalem. They saw how tenderly Joseph buried Him. Then they went home. They prepared spices and perfumes. On Saturday, the Sabbath, they rested. Very early Sunday morning they came to the tomb carrying their spices. They wanted to pour perfumes over Jesus' body and place the sweet spices in the folds of the linen wrap. They thought this was His final resting place.

- **If you had been a friend of the pilot, how would you have responded to his sudden appearance? What would you have wanted to do?**

_____

_____

_____

_____

_____

_____

_____

_____

1. **What was the angel's** *message to the women?*

_____

_____

_____

2. **How did the** *women react to what they saw and heard?*

_____

_____

_____

3. **If you had been** *there, what would you have thought about the angel's message?*

_____

_____

_____

The women knew that a huge, round stone covered the opening to the tomb. They wondered who would roll it away for them. When they arrived at the grave, they were astonished to find that the stone was rolled to one side. They also heard remarkable news from God's messenger.

Resurrection Victory

In Jesus' resurrection, God conquered death for us. Jesus has destroyed its power. Death could not hold Him in the grave. He overcame death, our last great enemy.

The resurrection of Jesus was a sign from God. By that great miracle, He announced that His plan to save people from sin was completed. The death and resurrection of Jesus brought us forgiveness of sin. God gave His approval to all that Jesus had done in His suffering and sacrifice. Where God grants forgiveness for sin, He grants eternal life and salvation.

Our last great enemy is death. We deserve to be cut off eternally from God because we have sinned. Adam's sin of rebellion against God has become our own sin. That is the message of God's Law. Our sin condemns us.

Jesus is God's Second Adam. He brought life to us when He overcame death for us. Now we no longer need to fear death. Our risen and living Savior will take us by the hand. He will raise us up at the Last Day and lead us, together with all the faithful, to the eternal presence of God the Father. That is the Good News of the Gospel.

God brought Israel out of slavery in Egypt. God has brought us out of the dark slavery of death into the light of life through the resurrection of His Son. The Law shows us our sin and our slavery to it. The Gospel shows us our Savior and His work to save us. Our faith and hope are fixed on God, who raised Jesus from the dead and gave us life and salvation. Our Baptism reminds us of Jesus' resurrection victory for us. Each day as we receive forgiveness, our old nature is drowned and dies so that the new person God has made us in Christ can come forth and live for God. Because of Jesus' death and resurrection, we are slaves to sin no more!

- **My prayer to Christ for His resurrection victory:**

_____

_____

_____

Sign: _____

Date: _____

Talk about it With My Family

- **As a family,** talk about things that make you happy (e.g., balloons, butterflies, confetti, brightly colored banners, noisemakers). Things that make us happy remind us of Jesus' victory over death—the greatest reason of all to celebrate and be happy. Share the Gospel with one another.

- **Talk about** a recent time when members of your family were angry with one another. Describe your thoughts and feelings. What Law messages were given? How did the power of Christ's forgiveness change your hearts and minds? What Gospel messages were given?

With My Mentor

- **Discuss together** what knowing God's forgiveness means to you. What difference does peace with God through Jesus make in your life?

- **If you are** having trouble forgiving someone or believing God's forgiveness for you, ask your mentor for suggestions on what you can do. Talk about what Law and Gospel messages are appropriate in each situation.

29

Jesus Ascends into Heaven

The Second Article

I believe . . . in Jesus Christ, His only Son, our Lord, who was conceived by the Holy Spirit, born of the Virgin Mary, suffered under Pontius Pilate, was crucified, died and was buried. He descended into hell. The third day He rose again from the dead. He ascended into heaven and sits at the right hand of God, the Father Almighty. From thence He will come to judge the living and the dead.

What does this mean? I believe that Jesus Christ, true God, begotten of the Father from eternity, and also true man, born of the Virgin Mary, is my Lord, who has redeemed me, a lost and condemned person, purchased and won me from all sins, from death, and from the power of the devil; not with gold or silver, but with His holy, precious blood and with His innocent suffering and death, that I may be His own and live under Him in His kingdom and serve Him in everlasting righteousness, innocence, and blessedness, just as He is risen from the dead, lives and reigns to all eternity. This is most certainly true.

Farewell

The forty days after Jesus rose from the dead were exciting days for the disciples. Jesus would suddenly appear in their midst and then just as suddenly disappear again! They did not know when or where to expect Him next. Jesus was teaching them how to get along without His visible presence. Yet He wanted them to be sure that He was alive again after His crucifixion.

After His suffering, He showed Himself to these men and gave many convincing proofs that He was alive. He appeared to them over a period of forty days and spoke about the kingdom of God. On one occasion, while He was eating with them, He gave them this command: "Do not leave Jerusalem, but wait for the gift My Father promised, which you have heard Me speak about. For John baptized with water, but in a few days you will be baptized with the Holy Spirit."

So when they met together, they asked Him, "Lord, are You at this time going to restore the kingdom to Israel?"

He said to them: "It is not for you to know the times or dates the Father has set by His own authority. But you will receive power when the Holy Spirit comes on you; and you will be My witnesses in Jerusalem, and in all Judea and Samaria, and to the ends of the earth."

After He said this, He was taken up before their very eyes, and a cloud hid Him from their sight. They were looking intently up into the sky as He was going, when suddenly two men dressed in white stood beside them. "Men of Galilee," they said, "why do you stand here looking into the sky? This same Jesus, who has been taken from you into heaven, will come back in the same way you have seen Him go into heaven."

Acts 1:3–11

One day, on top of a hill, Jesus spoke to His disciples again. He raised His hands to bless His disciples. As He did this, He slowly rose into the sky. His disciples watched in wonder as they saw Him rise. Soon a cloud covered Him completely, but they still kept looking into the sky, perhaps hoping to see Him again.

- **What promise and commission did Jesus give to His disciples?**

_____

_____

_____

Christ with Us

After His resurrection, Jesus stayed on earth to minister to His disciples for forty days. When He ascended into heaven, He continued to rule the whole world from His throne at the right hand of God. He left so that He could carry out His promise to send the Holy Spirit, the Comforter.

Even though Jesus visibly left the earth, He was still with His disciples. He was with them through the work of the Holy Spirit. The Holy Spirit gave them the faith to believe that Jesus was truly present with them and the wisdom and courage to be His witnesses.

Jesus is present with His disciples today. He is present in His Word, in Baptism, and in the Holy Supper. We cannot see Jesus, just as His disciples could not see Him after His ascension. The Holy Spirit gives Jesus' disciples today the same power He gave the first disciples. Jesus still rules the whole world from His throne at the right hand of God. He equips us to follow Him and to share His Good News.

Jesus promises to be with His disciples today, giving them the wisdom and courage to share the Gospel with others.

- **Describe and give examples that show Jesus is with you in your life.**

_____

_____

_____

He Will Come Again

The angels told the disciples that Jesus would return to the earth, but they did not tell them when that would be. Scripture tells us that the same Jesus who ascended into heaven will come in person to earth again. He will come in glory and honor to raise the dead and gather God's people for eternal life. He is now at God's right hand, ruling the world; at His second coming He will openly reveal to all that He is Lord.

Will we know Him when He returns? Yes! Everyone will see Him and recognize Him as the Lord. In the meantime, Christians tell others the Good News of salvation and help others. When we love others, we love Jesus too.

God has already appointed the day when Christ will return. Since He has not told anyone when it is to be, we live each day trusting His grace to save us. While we wait, we share the Gospel with people everywhere, so that they, too, can live with Him forever in heaven.

My Prayer

- **I ask You, risen Lord Jesus,**

_____

_____

_____

_____

Sign: _____

Date: _____

 **Talk about it** With My Family

- **Mark Ascension Day** on your family calendar. Plan to do something outdoors that day. Go to the top of a high-rise building or to a high geographic point in your area. Bring a Bible and read the ascension story from Acts 1.

- **Identify people** who do not know Jesus as their Savior. Plan a way your family could witness to them about Jesus' love and forgiveness. Pray for that individual or family during the week, and invite them to a worship service or another activity at your church.

With My Mentor

- **Plan a personal** devotional schedule for each day of the next week. Follow your plan. Then discuss how having devotions helps you remember that Jesus is always with you, as He promised.

- **Learn more about** a missionary family. Discuss ways you can support their ministry.

30

Jesus Sends the Holy Spirit

When the day of Pentecost came, they were all together in one place. Suddenly a sound like the blowing of a violent wind came from heaven and filled the whole house where they were sitting. They saw what seemed to be tongues of fire that separated and came to rest on each of them. All of them were filled with the Holy Spirit and began to speak in other tongues as the Spirit enabled them.

Now there were staying in Jerusalem God-fearing Jews from every nation under heaven. When they heard this sound, a crowd came together in bewilderment, because each one heard them speaking in his own language. Utterly amazed, they asked: "Are not all these men who are speaking Galileans?" . . .

Some, however, made fun of them and said, "They have had too much wine."

Then Peter stood up with the Eleven, raised his voice and addressed the crowd: "Fellow Jews and all of you who live in Jerusalem, let me explain this to you; listen carefully to what I say. These men are not drunk, as you suppose. It's only nine in the morning! No, this is what was spoken by the prophet Joel:

" 'In the last days, God says, I will pour out My Spirit on all people.' "

Acts 2:1–7, 13–17

The Third Article

I believe in the Holy Spirit, the holy Christian church, the communion of saints, the forgiveness of sins, the resurrection of the body, and the life everlasting. Amen.

What does this mean? I believe that I cannot by my own reason or strength believe in Jesus Christ, my Lord, or come to Him; but the Holy Spirit has called me by the Gospel, enlightened me with His gifts, sanctified and kept me in the true faith. In the same way He calls, gathers, enlightens, and sanctifies the whole Christian church on earth, and keeps it with Jesus Christ in the one true faith. In this Christian church He daily and richly forgives all my sins and the sins of all believers. On the Last Day He will raise me and all the dead, and give eternal life to me and all believers in Christ. This is most certainly true.

Pentecost in Jerusalem

Ten days had passed since the disciples watched Jesus ascend into heaven. They were waiting in Jerusalem, as Jesus had told them to do. They remembered His promise to send them the Holy Spirit and power. How would God keep His promise? How would the Holy Spirit come to them?

The city of Jerusalem was filled with travelers and strangers from many lands. It was the Festival of Pentecost. Thousands of people had come to Jerusalem from all over the world to celebrate this festival.

Then it happened! First, there was a noise. It was like a mighty wind blowing down the streets. This loud sound led crowds of people to the house where the disciples were assembled in prayer. Small flames of fire appeared, separated, and came to rest on the disciples. They began to speak in other languages! Many people were amazed to hear these Galileans speak.

Simon Peter believed that the Holy Spirit had come. He began to preach about this great miracle. He spoke about the crucifixion and resurrection of Jesus and reminded the people that they had put Jesus on the cross. "What shall we do?" they asked. "Repent and be baptized," he told them, "and you will receive the gift of the Holy Spirit."

God kept His promise to send the Holy Spirit to the disciples. Pentecost was the day the Spirit came. Through the Word and Baptism, the Holy Spirit gathers many people into the Church of Jesus Christ.

Christ's Church is present when people gather regularly to hear the Gospel and to celebrate the Sacraments.

- **How would you summarize Peter's sermon? Check out Acts 2:14–41. Then write a short summary.**

_____

_____

_____

_____

_____

_____

_____

_____

_____

_____

_____

My Journey in Faith

Our study of the Christian faith has explored the history of God's plan of salvation for sinful people. It is the story of our mighty and gracious God at work. Through God's Word, the Holy Spirit has taught us that God sent His Son, Jesus, to rescue sinners from eternal death and to give His people eternal life. It is an unfinished history, for it includes us today.

God's saving activity began when God spoke His promise to Adam and Eve. It continued when God chose Abraham to be the father of many nations and when God rescued His people from slavery in Egypt.

When God's people, Israel, sinned and disobeyed, God took them from the land promised to them to exile in another land. Yet His steadfast love watched carefully over the remnant of His people who believed. He sent His prophets to proclaim His new covenant to them. Finally, from this remnant of people God brought forth His only Son.

Jesus, born of Mary, is the long-promised Messiah, the Second Adam. Jesus, in His life on earth, displayed the power of almighty God. He healed the sick, gave sight to the blind, raised the dead, and proclaimed the Gospel of peace. He lived a perfect life in our place. He conquered all of our enemies: sin, Satan, and death. He fulfilled all the prophecies given in the Old Testament about the Messiah. He kept God's Law perfectly. He was obedient, even dying for us. He is the Lamb of God who takes away the sin of the world. In Jesus' resurrection, God completed His work, His plan of salvation. One great event is still to come. On the Last Day, Jesus will return in glory to judge the living and the dead.

Before He ascended into heaven, Jesus gathered His disciples together for one last message. He commanded them to be witnesses of His Word and work. He told them to make disciples of all nations. He gave them the Sacraments of Baptism and Holy Communion as His means of grace. Christ founded the Church at Pentecost when He sent the Holy Spirit.

In Holy Baptism, Jesus calls sinners into His kingdom. We are His new people in the world. All disciples of Jesus Christ form the community of the Church: people who glorify and praise God as they speak the Word of God's forgiveness to each other and to the world.

This is our call today: to continue to make disciples of all nations by proclaiming the Good News of God's great work of salvation in Jesus Christ. Because our heavenly Father has loved us, we show His love for others in words and in deeds. In this way, God's Holy Spirit is at work in today's world through His Church.

- **Write a prayer talking to God about what the gift of His Spirit means to you.**

_____

_____

_____

_____

_____

_____

Sign: _____

Date: _____

Talk about it With My Family

- **After a family** meal, set a candle in the middle of the table and light it. Read 2 Timothy 1:5. Invite each member to thank God for someone who has shared the Christian faith with your family.

- **Identify another** family in your neighborhood with whom you can share God's love in Christ. Extend an invitation to them to join you for worship at your church.

With My Mentor

- **Ask your mentor** how he or she has had an opportunity to witness to Jesus at home and at work. Talk about difficulties that you face in sharing your faith. Pray together, asking for the Holy Spirit's strengthening.

- **Discuss how you** and your mentor can keep contact in the years ahead. Perhaps you can make contact on your birthdays. Write a thank-you note to your mentor for the help you have received during your study of My Journey in Faith.